THE DISSIDENT PRESS

The SAGE CommText Series

Editor:
F. GERALD KLINE
Director, School of Journalism and Mass Communication
University of Minnesota

Associate Editor:
SUSAN H. EVANS
Annenberg School of Communications,
University of Southern California

This new series of communication textbooks is designed to provide a modular approach to teaching in this rapidly changing area. The explosion of concepts, methodologies, levels of analysis, and philosophical perspectives has put heavy demands on teaching undergraduates and graduates alike; it is our intent to choose the most solidly argued of these to make them available for students and teachers. The addition of new titles in the CommText series as well as the presentation of new and diverse authors will be a continuing effort on our part to reflect change in this scholarly area.

—F.G.K. and S.H.E.

additional titles in preparation

Lauren Kessler

⌈THE DISSIDENT PRESS⌋

Alternative Journalism in American History

Volume 13. The Sage COMMTEXT Series

SAGE PUBLICATIONS
Beverly Hills / London / New Delhi

For information address:

SAGE Publications, Inc.
275 South Beverly Drive
Beverly Hills, California 90212

SAGE Publications India Pvt. Ltd.
C-236 Defence Colony
New Delhi 110 024, India

SAGE Publications Ltd
28 Banner Street
London EC1Y 8QE, England

Printed in the United States of America

Library of Congress Cataloging in Publication Data

Main entry under title:

Kessler, Lauren.
    The dissident press.

    (Sage commtext series; v. 13)
    1. Underground press—United States—History.
2. Ethnic press—United States—History. 3. Press and
politics—United States—History. 4. Radicalism—United
States. 5. Dissenters—United States. I. Title. II. Series
PN4888.U5K47   071'.3   83-21112
ISBN 0-8039-2086-5
ISBN 0-8039-2087-3 (pbk.)

FIRST PRINTING

CONTENTS

ACKNOWLEDGMENTS

It is invariably the busiest people who manage to find time to help their colleagues, and I am indebted to several of these harried souls. Everette Dennis, dean of the University of Oregon's School of Journalism, read the entire manuscript, offering insightful comments and more than a few helpful suggestions. I thank him not only for this but for his support and encouragement throughout the project. Marion Marzolf at the University of Michigan also reviewed the manuscript, and I thank her for her careful comments and kind support. Without the enthusiasm of Susan Evans at the University of Southern California, this project might still be on seven floppy disks. I owe her much for believing in the project and me.

I am also indebted to Profs. Bill Ames, Jerry Baldasty, and Roger Simpson at the University of Washington for helping me hone the skills that made the writing of this book possible. They will recognize their influence in Chapter 1. A summer research grant from the University of Oregon Graduate School helped greatly in the beginning stages of this work.

This book is dedicated to Tom for all the usual reasons and many more.

—L.K.

1

OTHER VOICES

What is essential is not that everyone shall speak, but that everything worth saying shall be heard.
—Alexander Meiklejohn

What should a free press be free to do? Does the freedom granted the press by the First Amendment carry with it certain responsibilities? Should a free press mean more than protection for those who own the channels of communication? Philosophers, historians, legal thinkers, and generations of working journalists and their concerned publics have grappled with these questions.

And they are grappling still. No widely accepted or enforced set of guidelines presents a blueprint for the operation of our institutions of mass communication. The First Amendment states that the press should be free to operate without government interference. But free to operate *how*?

First Amendment theorist Alexander Meiklejohn, quoted at the beginning of this chapter, believes a free press should include diverse ideas—"everything worth saying"—and should encourage this diversity. These are the responsibilities imposed by freedom. What Meiklejohn, and many others before and after him, is talking about is a concept that has long figured prominently in communications history and law: *the marketplace of ideas*. The press, say believers in this concept, ought to operate as an open forum for the exchange of ideas, a marketplace that presents the public with a diversity of theories, thoughts, sentiments, and opinions. The public meanders through the marketplace (by reading, listening, or viewing the mass media), "buys" (accepts, agrees with) certain ideas, and rejects others. The marketplace of ideas is in no way a blueprint for the operation of the mass media, but it is a powerful concept that suggests some of the responsibilities of a free press.

THE MARKETPLACE OF IDEAS

The free marketplace of ideas refers to several interrelated concepts of free speech:

— the basic First Amendment freedoms that allow the marketplace to function: the freedom to speak and the freedom to listen (peaceable assembly);
— the existence and toleration of a diversity of ideas and opinions within the free press;
— the encouragement of diversity (by equitably granting access to the marketplace for diverse, even unpopular, ideas);
— the belief that open discussion of a diversity of ideas will eventually result in the triumph of truth and those ideas that are right for society at the time.

As long ago as the seventeenth century, essayist John Milton articulated the keystone of the free marketplace concept when he wrote:

Though all the winds of doctrine were let loose to play upon the earth, so truth be in the field, we do injuriously by licensing and prohibiting to misdoubt her strength. Let [truth] and falsehood grapple; who ever knew truth put to the worse, in a free and open encounter?

In Milton's marketplace, all ideas—good and bad, truth and lies—could battle one another. After a fair fight, said Milton, truth would triumph.

The nineteenth-century philosopher John Stuart Mill also argued for tolerance of contrary opinions within the marketplace:

If all mankind minus one, were of one opinion, and only one person were of the contrary opinion, mankind would be no more justified in silencing that one person than he, if he had the power, would be justified in silencing mankind.

In post-World War II America, a group of distinguished intellectuals who called themselves the Commission on Freedom of the Press echoed Milton's and Mills' defense of minority views:

> Valuable ideas may be put forth first in forms that are crude, indefensible, or even dangerous. They need the chance to develop through free criticism as well as the chance to survive on the basis of ultimate worth.

Dubbed the Hutchins Commission after the man who headed the enterprise, University of Chicago's chancellor Dr. Robert Maynard Hutchins, the group submitted its guidelines for the operation of a free and responsible press in 1947. The press, wrote the commission, ought to provide

— a truthful, comprehensive, intelligent account of the day's events in a context that gives them meaning;
— a forum for expressions on all sides of an issue;
— the projection of a representative picture of the constituent groups in the society, portraying conflicting groups fairly, without stereotypes based on a few incidents or individuals;
— the presentation and clarification of the goals and values of the society; and
— full access to the day's intelligence.

The First Amendment, wrote the commission, "was intended to guarantee free expression, not to create a privileged industry." Commission members, as well as other twentieth-century critics, stressed the importance of participation by all in the marketplace of ideas. Participation should not depend on personal or corporate wealth. Indeed they insisted that corporate power ought to be blunted to create the conditions under which individuals and minority groups could champion their ideas.

The courts, particularly in the twentieth century, have also supported the concept of the free marketplace. Justice Brandeis wrote in 1927 that the freedom "to think as you will and to speak as you think" was essential to the search for political truth. Although freedom of speech meant that some false or erroneous information would be part of public discussion, Brandeis believed this did not warrant government intervention to prevent or punish falsity. "If there be a time to expose through discussion the falsehoods and fallacies . . . the remedy to be applied is more speech, not enforced silence."

A more recent defender of the free marketplace, Justice Hugo Black, insisted that a diversity of ideas within the press was necessary for public welfare and a democratic society. The First Amendment, wrote Black in an antitrust case against the Associated Press, "rests on the assumption that the widest possible dissemination of information from diverse and antagonistic sources is essential to the welfare of the public, that a free press is a condition of a free society."

In theory, then, the marketplace of our democratic heritage operates by only a few rules:

— All ideas, although not necessarily all individuals, should have access to the forum.
— What is said (or printed) may be true or false. It may be selfishly or magnanimously motivated. (People, however, may be held responsible for falsehoods after publication.)
— If the government has a role in regulating the marketplace, it is only to ensure two conditions: (1) that access to the marketplace is free and (2) that the diversity inherent in society is mirrored in the marketplace.

Although the free marketplace concept has been written about for centuries and at times has been defended vigorously in the courts, some critics argue that it has never actually existed. Political scientist John Roche believes America never had a tradition of libertarianism, of an open exchange of ideas from divergent or dissenting sources. While it may appear that an open forum for ideas existed, says Roche, a closer look at history shows that libertarianism is a myth.

America in the seventeenth and eighteenth centuries, says Roche, was an open society dotted with closed enclaves where one could settle with cobelievers and oppress or ostracize dissenters. Because there was room for physical expansion, the dissenters were free to leave and start their own enclave where they, in turn, could oppress or ostracize *their* dissenters. Each enclave was a closed marketplace in which divergent ideas were not tolerated. Diversity came from the proliferation of separate, closed marketplaces. In urban America of the late nineteenth and twentieth centuries, Roche sees freedom of expression as a function of impersonalization and the growth of instituitions that muffle intergroup conflict. Nowhere does he see a tradition of tolerance for or encouragement of diverse ideas within a national forum.

Legal scholar Jerome Barron concedes that a free marketplace may have existed during the eighteenth-century heyday of political pamphleteering, but says today it is a "romantic conception." The mass media, says Barron, have developed an antipathy to ideas, and legal intervention is needed if new or unpopular ideas are to be assured a forum.

What both Roche and Barron point to when they suggest a free marketplace does not exist is the media's lack of tolerance for dissenting, divergent, or unpopular ideas. At the heart of the free marketplace is this diversity. The existence, toleration, and encouragement of diversity is central to both Milton's and Mills' ideas and is explicitly stated in the Hutchins Commission report. To have diversity, the marketplace must be open to all who want to participate. The marketplace—the press—must grant access to a variety of ideas.

ACCESS

"There's freedom of the press for the guy who owns one," journalist A. J. Leibling once quipped. Several decades later, Barron turned this witticism into an imperative: "Freedom of the press must mean something more than a guarantee of the property rights of media owners." Implicit in these two comments is the notion that certain people, groups, and ideas have routinely been denied access to the marketplace of the conventional, established press. Barron maintains that the media stifle unpopular ideas and refuse access to both minorities and groups working for social and political change.

Reports from those involved in such groups lend credence to Barron's criticism. Muckraking journalist, novelist, and politician Upton Sinclair, in *The Brass Check*, painstakingly detailed his experience as a socialist writer with what he called "the privileged press." He maintained that news channels became "concrete walls" when he attempted to publish exposés of the horrors of industrial capitalism. Susan B. Anthony, one of the leaders of the fight for women's right to vote, wrote that it was impossible to secure space in any newspaper for woman suffrage arguments. The nineteenth-century press, she said, regularly referred to suffragists as "hyenas, cats, crowing hens, bold wantons, unsexed females and dangerous homewreckers."

Throughout our history, Black Americans have criticized the press for either ignoring them and their pleas for equality or for ridiculing them. When Samuel Cornish and John Russwurm, two Black freemen, wanted to respond to a series of racial attacks in several New York City newspapers, they were told the marketplace was closed to their ideas.

Of course, those in the midst of unpopular political battles might be expected to criticize the press for excluding or ridiculing their ideas. They are perhaps not the most dispassionate evaluators of media performance. But historians, far from the heat of the moment, also suggest that the ideas and goals of certain groups have been denied access to the marketplace. In *Slavery,* Stanley Elkins writes of the Abolitionists' futile attempts to disseminate their ideas through the popular press. The Populists, a vast organization of southern and western farmers fighting for economic reform in the last quarter of the nineteenth century, also had problems gaining access to the media marketplace. The press, writes Lawrence Goodwin in *The Democratic Promise,* was in step with current economic dogma and tightly bound to the two-party system. The novel ideas of the Populists were unacceptable. The press generally ignored the Populists, but when it did comment on the group's ideas, it foresook discussion for diatribe. Pacifists and noninterventionists prior to World War I experienced the same problem, according to two historians of the era. Denied access to all but a few large circulation dailies, those who believed America should not enter the war searched in vain for a way to put their ideas before the public. Their unpopular cause, conclude Peterson and Fite in *Opponents of War,* received scant attention.

The evidence—both from those directly involved in unpopular causes and from those, years or centuries later, who analyzed the events—overwhelmingly points to a closed marketplace within the popular conventional press. Participation—access—has been routinely denied to those who held aberrant beliefs. This lack of access has taken at least three forms:

(1) complete exclusion from the popular media marketplace of the group, its ideas and goals;
(2) exclusion of ideas, goals, and programs of the group, but inclusion of events (e.g., marches, strikes, demonstrations) in which the group participated;
(3) ridicule, insult, or stereotyping of the group and its ideas rather than discussion, explanation, and debate.

Merely mentioning a group does not constitute access. What the group stands for, what it is fighting for (or against)—its ideas—also must receive a forum. Whatever the type of lack of access, the result is the same: Ideas are denied their place in the popular forum; groups are denied full participation in the marketplace; and the public is denied, in the words of the Hutchins Commission, "a representative picture of the constituent groups in the society."

REDISCOVERING THE MARKETPLACE

If we look at only the well-established, conventional institutions of mass communication, we will not often find a free and open exchange of ideas. If we look only at the popular press, we will get little feeling for the richness, complexity, and conflict that have always been a part of American society. For historically the conventional press has spoken to and for the homogeneous middle. Not only has it not attempted to be "all things for all people," it has been one of the chief defenders of the status quo. It has created a marketplace closed to all but those who hold beliefs and ideas consistent with what is currently acceptable.

Yet Blacks, suffragists, Populists, socialists, and others who professed aberrant beliefs were heard, not in the closed marketplace of the conventional press but in the marketplace of their own creation. It is these marketplaces—the thousands of publications created and sustained by those who do not represent the homogeneous middle—that collectively present the marketplace of ideas.

Perhaps we need to redefine and rediscover this marketplace. The new social history, sometimes called "history from the bottom up," can provide the necessary framework. Traditional history, like traditional press history, attempts to define an era by relying on the views and action of leaders. It is "history from the top down." Within this construct, press history becomes the narrative of Dana, Bennett, Raymond, Hearst, and Pulitzer—the leaders and the media institutions they led. It becomes the history of the conventional marketplace that granted access to a small spectrum of acceptable ideas.

But the new social history looks at people, not leaders. It emphasizes human, not institutional voices. Within this framework, press history may become an investigation of those people whose efforts are part of our journalistic heritage but who were not part of the institutional mainstream. By looking at press history from the bottom up we can rediscover a complex marketplace of ideas in the passionate rhetoric of the dispossessed.

DISSIDENT VOICES

This book investigates a handful of the many fringe groups—political, social, and cultural—who, denied access to the mainstream media marketplace, started marketplaces of their own. This was, many of the participants believed, the only way their voices could be heard. It is important to note that many of the dissident marketplaces were no more free and open than the conventional media. These separate marketplaces often mirrored John Roche's concept of free expression in early America. The dissidents, unable to gain a fair hearing for their ideas in the established media of their time, set off to create their own newspapers and periodicals. But often these marketplaces were closed to ideas and opinions at odds with the group. Nowhere is this more evident than in the socialist and communist press of the late nineteenth and early twentieth centuries where there was an almost astounding proliferation of closed marketplaces. Groups splintered. Splinter groups splintered, and splintered again. Each group, some containing no more than a dozen members, published its own journal.

The journalistic efforts of six groups are explored in these pages: Black Americans; utopians and communitarians; feminists; non-English-speaking immigrants; Populists, anarchists, socialists, communists, and their splinter groups;

and pacifists, noninterventionists, and resisters during World War I, World War II, and Vietnam.

These groups share a number of traits. They were the underdogs of their time. All held views or believed in ideas that diverged from the mainstream political, economic, social, and cultural climate of their times. All wanted, to some degree, to effect social change. All wanted access to the popular media marketplace for their ideas, or sometimes merely for their existence as a group. All were excluded from the conventional marketplace, although the extent and type of exclusion (denial of access) varied from group to group and over time. In response to this exclusion—and because the groups wanted to disseminate their ideas to a larger public—they started media marketplaces of their own. Thousands of newspapers—from large-circulation dailies to tiny, struggling weeklies—and hundreds of magazines, journals, special interest publications, and quarterlies were part of these marketplaces. All six groups had one more trait in common: Their ideas, over time, filtered into the mainstream marketplace. And several of these ideas, notably Black equality and female political participation, evolved from radical, unpopular, even ridiculed notions to accepted political doctrine.

These groups were chosen for reasons other than their commonalities. Because they span more than a century and a half, from the early 1800s to the late 1900s, they show that the presence of alternative voices in America is a *tradition,* not a time-bound phenomenon. This idea—that there is and has always been an operational alternative press—is vital to both our appreciation of the richness of journalism history and our understanding of the complexity of the marketplace.

Unlike short-lived special interest groups or groups whose ideas quickly became accepted into the mainstream marketplace, these groups struggled for years. During their struggle they produced an impressive variety and number of publications. The wealth of publications started by these groups is another reason they were included in this study.

Finally, these groups were chosen because they represent at least some of the diversity found in American society: the upper-crust Bostonians who met in parlors to discuss transcendentalism, the powerless Blacks and women who fought for political recognition, the poor farmers of the South and West, the millions of ethnically diverse immigrants in America's urban centers, the working-class intellectuals who looked abroad for political ideologies.

Black Americans

"The *Sun* shines for all white men and not for colored men," stated a *New York Sun* editorial in 1847. Twenty years earlier, a northern Black had started the first Black newspaper after the New York press refused to print his article. Throughout the pre-Civil War era Black (and white) abolitionists found it necessary to create their own marketplace in order to spread ideas of Black enfranchisement and equality. After the war and after the slaves were freed, the access problem remained. Hundreds of Black newspapers, magazines, and special interest periodicals continued to be founded, and maintained, by Blacks who believed the conventional press belittled, ridiculed, or ignored them. Even after Blacks became part of the mainstream in post-World War II America, they continued to sustain their own media marketplace. The second chapter chronicles the voices of Black Americans.

Utopians and Communitarians

From the founding of what Puritans called "The City of the Hill" to the establishment of Stephen Gaskin's Farm in the 1960s, Americans have experimented with "intentional communities." Dissatisfied with the norms and values of conventional society, these seekers invented and reinvented their vision of utopia. But for many it was not enough to live the vision; they must also spread the word. Excluded from all but a few mainstream publications, the utopians began their own press: *Oneida Circular* published by John Noyes' Oneida Community, *New Harmony Gazette* from Robert Owens' New Harmony settlement, *The Harbinger* from the Brook Farm experiment, and hundreds of other newspapers and periodicals representing utopian experiments across the nation. The third chapter discusses this tradition of "new age" journalism, which was still alive in the 1970s in the pages of *Communities, Seriatim,* and *The Whole Earth Catalog.*

Feminists

"We have begun a siege of the citadels of one-sexed govern-ment," wrote an Oregon suffragist in the first issue of her weekly newspaper. "We will continue with unabated persistency." Excluded from the political and economic life of their country, denied access to the conventional press of their day, American women did continue their fight for the right to vote with unabated persistency. Beginning in the 1840s and culminating with the passage of the Nineteenth Amendment in 1920, the fight for female enfranchisement raged nationwide and included numerous suffrage newspapers and periodicals. In the twentieth century, women have continued to battle stereo-typing and exclusion from, or underrepresentation in, the political and professional spheres through the pages of their own publications. The fourth chapter chronicles and discusses the journalistic efforts of all these women.

Immigrants

Pulitzer prize-winning historian Oscar Handlin called them "the uprooted." They were the nineteenth- and early twentieth-century immigrants who came from the quiet villages of Europe to the urban wilderness of America's metropolises. The conven-tional press—even the so-called popular press—failed to meet their needs. Often these strangers would not read an English-language paper, and even if they could, they rarely found their concerns reflected in its pages. Ignored, stereotyped, sometimes ridiculed, these immigrants developed their own alternative press. In dozens of languages in dozens of American cities and towns, the foreign language press flourished and still flourishes today. The fifth chapter discusses and evaluates the immigrant press and how it served and continues to serve the needs of its special public.

Populists, Anarchists, Socialists, and Communists

The idea that "plain people"—workers—could work together to gain control of their own lives and their own futures was at the heart of a variety of American radical movements. Populism, a powerful third-party movement of farmers in the West, South, and Midwest, called for a reordering of the national economy. Anarchists, socialists, and communists fought against what they called the absolute privilege of owners and for the rights of the working class. The ideas and goals of these radical groups went against the grain of mainstream society. To be heard, they had to establish their own press. Gathering steam in the 1870s, by 1892 the Populist movement boasted more than 900 newspapers. Anarchists, socialists, communists, and their dizzying variety of splinter groups published more than 600 newspapers and periodicals in the early 1900s. The sixth chapter explores this volatile alternative press.

War Resisters

During the hysteria of 1917-1918, the aggressive patriotism following Pearl Harbor and the chauvinism of the mid-1960s, the conventional press almost unanimously supported American war efforts. But what of those who did not—the pacifists, the noninterventionists, the soldiers who found they could not obey? These people started their own newspapers. Hounded under the Espionage Act of 1917, called "Hitler's henchmen" during World War II, harassed and sometimes jailed during the Vietnam war, these resisters and their journalistic efforts were a vital part of press history. Their efforts are considered in Chapter 7.

Each of these chapters presents the historical context for the group and discusses the formation of its press and the goals and objectives of these dissident journalists. Their difficulties— economic, political, and personal—are chronicled. Over time, many of these groups had an impact on both conventional thinking and the conventional press. This too is discussed.

These groups represent only a small portion of the perhaps hundreds of organized dissident groups who have been a part of American society and American journalism. Eighteenth-century American revolutionaries, religious dissidents of all stripes, Native Americans, conservationists and environmentalists, rightwing organizations like the Ku Klux Klan, cultural radicals of the 1960s—all these and many more could easily be included in a study of the alternative press. There are many more voices to document in the redefined marketplace.

For regardless of the closed enclave of the conventional press, regardless of government or citizen harassment, critics, dissenters, and nonconformists have existed—and sometimes thrived—on the fringes of American society. Free speech may not mean a free and open marketplace of ideas within the conventional press, but it has meant the freedom to expand the marketplace—and, ultimately, the freedom to speak.

REFERENCES

The following material aided in the preparation of this chapter and is suggested for further reading:

Barron, Jerome A. *Freedom of the Press for Whom?* Bloomington: Indiana University Press, 1973.
Bosmajian, Haig A., ed. *The Principles and Practice of Freedom of Speech.* Boston: Houghton Mifflin, 1971.
The Commission on Freedom of the Press. *A Free and Responsible Press.* Chicago: University of Chicago Press, 1947.
Meiklejohn, Alexander. *Political Freedom.* New York: Harper & Brothers, 1948.
Roche, John. *Shadow and Substance.* New York: Macmillan, 1964.
Roshco, Bernard. *Newsmaking.* Chicago: University of Chicago Press, 1975.
Schmidt, Benno C. *Freedom of the Press v. Public Access.* New York: Praeger, 1976.

2

THE FREEDOM TRAIN

We wish to plead our cause. Too long have others spoken for us. Too long has the public been deceived by misrepresentations in the things that concern us dearly.

—*Freedom's Journal*

With this polite but impassioned statement of editorial purpose, the nation's first Black newspaper began publication. The year was 1827, 137 years after the appearance of the first white newspaper in the colonies and almost two generations before Blacks were freed from the bonds of slavery. *Freedom's Journal,* produced by and for Blacks, was the first of the more than 2,700 newspapers, magazines, and quarterly journals that have comprised Black journalism in America.

Originating both because and in spite of adversity, the Black press has had a rich, varied, volatile history. It is the story of persistent struggle against widespread cultural prejudice mirrored by stereotyping and rejection in the conventional white media. It is the story of powerless, often penniless men and women who devoted their energies, and sometimes risked their lives, in hopes of bettering the condition of their race. The journalistic effort of Blacks is one part—one very important part—of the political and economic struggle for equality that continues today.

THE PROBLEM OF ACCESS

When a relatively small group of people on the fringes of society wants to make its presence known, when it wants to expound on its goals and ideas in hopes of affecting political or societal change, its first choice is to use the conventional channels of mass communication. Through well-established, mass circulation media the group can reach the widest, most diverse audience with its message. This is what Black Americans and their leaders hoped for: a forum in the mainstream press. But the mainstream press was, by and large, unresponsive. The conventional media marketplace was—and to a great extent still is—closed to Blacks. It was this denial of access that spurred the growth of a separate Black press.

In the spring of 1827 two Black freemen read vile attacks against their race in the New York *Enquirer* and several other New York City newspapers. They responded immediately with letters to the editor. The letters were not published; nor were the two freemen's subsequent attempts to get their views in print. They would have preferred a diverse, citywide forum for their antislavery message. They settled for creating their own shoestring operation that would reach only a handful of subscribers, *Freedom's Journal.*

This scenario was repeated in city after city both before and after the Civil War. In 1843 a Black physician submitted a series of antislavery letters and articles to leading Pittsburgh newspapers. When the papers refused to print the articles, the physician started his own Abolitionist newspaper. Three years later, a Black freeman wrote a reply to a proslavery editorial in the New York *Sun*. The *Sun*, a popular Penny Press newspaper that attempted to appeal to the city's middle and working classes with the motto "The Sun Shines For All," refused to print the reply. Only after the writer paid $15 to have his letter printed as an advertisement, and only after the *Sun's* editors softened the comments in the letter, did it run in the newspaper. "The *Sun* shines for all *white* men," the writer was told, "and not for colored men."

Even after the U.S. government recognized Blacks as citizens, white newspapers continued as closed marketplaces reflecting entrenched racial prejudice. In 1863, one fanatical New York newspaper carried this motto under its masthead: "I hold that this government was made on the WHITE BASIS by WHITE MEN for the benefit of WHITE MEN and THEIR POSTERITY FOREVER." Most conventional publications were more circumspect about their exclusion of Blacks and the issues concerning them, but they excluded them nonetheless. Echoing the thoughts of his journalistic colleagues, Black editor T. Thomas Fortune wrote in 1890:

A sufficient answer to all those who do not understand why we have colored newspapers, would seem to be the fact that white men have newspapers; that they are published by white men for white men; give in the main news about white men, and pitch their editorial opinions entirely in the interest of white men.

When it did not ignore Blacks and their political, economic, and cultural goals, the white-owned press often stereotyped or ridiculed Black Americans. As late as 1947, a report written by nine Nieman Fellows at Harvard University claimed that newspapers in both the North and South were "consistently cruel to the colored man, patronizing him, keeping him in his place, thoughtlessly crucifying him in a thousand big and little ways." A year later the president of the editorial society of the Negro Publishers Association wrote that metropolitan newspapers "continue to play down Negro achievements while playing up Negro crime." These papers "persist in ignoring the cultural and social life of the Negro people," wrote Charles Loeb, and give only "passing thought to the Negro citizen as an American entity." Today's critics, both Black and white, fault the conventional press for the same shortcomings.

The Black press emerged as a response to the closed marketplace of ideas in the conventional press. In the new marketplace of their own making, Blacks fought against prejudice and discrimination and for full citizenship rights. Their publications, which began as reactions to the denial of access by the conventional press, grew to be independent forums that met the changing needs of their constituencies by providing information, education, and inspiration.

FUNCTIONS OF THE BLACK PRESS

In both pre- and post-Civil War America, Black leaders viewed their publications as a way—some thought the only way—to tell their story as a race. How did Blacks live? What did they care about? What were their problems, their achievements? The white press surveyed the white environment; if Black people wanted to know about themselves, they had to read their separate publications.

When the (New York) *Weekly Anglo-African* began publication in 1859, its editor offered this statement of purpose: "We need a press—a press of our own. We need to know something else of ourselves through the press than the everyday statements made up to suit the feelings . . . of our opponents." Of course, the newspaper propagandized for the Abolition cause, as did all Black newspapers of the time, but it also offered readers a look at themselves: Black society and culture seen through the eyes of Blacks. "No outside tongue, however gifted in eloquence, can tell [our] story," continued the statement, "no outside eye, however penetrating, can see [our] wants." The *Weekly Anglo-African* editor was saying what many of his contemporaries felt: Not even the sympathetic white-owned Abolitionist press could tell the whole story of the Black condition.

Looking back on more than 50 years of Black press history, Black professor Frank Trigg commented in 1890, "Were it not for the Negro press, the country would be in comparatively total darkness as to the Negroes' real condition." This sentiment is echoed by scores of Black editors and leaders from the early nineteenth to the late twentieth centuries.

In surveying the Black environment for its readers, Black newspapers and magazines not only exposed the often deplorable conditions of Black life but also recognized the accomplishment of Black workers and thinkers. In doing so, these journals helped engender racial pride while offering a source of inspiration to their readers. Coverage of Black accomplishments helped instill a positive sense of the progress and future of Black people. And the existence of Black-owned and operated publications showed Blacks less fortunate than the editors and leaders that the possibilities for their own futures were not as limited as they might have thought. Writing in 1890, one Black physician maintained that "the achievements of the Afro-American editor have resulted in the unification of the Afro-American people and the development of race pride, as well as the proper diffusion of knowledge." He may not have been overstating the case. Certainly Black lecturers, educators, lawyers, scientists, and other professionals also did much to foster racial pride. But how were Black people to know of these accomplishments if not through the pages of their own newspapers and magazines? When the white press included news of Blacks, wrote one twentieth-century critic, it portrayed them as either "clowns or criminals."

The Black press not only showed its own (Black) readers the possibilities of the race, it also sent a clear message to white society. Although it is doubtful that more than a handful of whites actually read Black journals, some of the news reported in these publications must have filtered into white society through less formal channels. But perhaps more important, the Black press proved by its very existence that Blacks were not intellectually inferior to whites. If Blacks could write, edit, and publish their own newspapers and magazines, if they could run their own businesses, how could whites continue to believe in racial inferiority? The Black press, wrote the great Abolitionist and editor Frederick Douglass, "has demonstrated, in large measure, the mental and literary possibilities of the colored race."

Many Black editors saw themselves as educators as well as journalists. Particularly before the Civil War, when many states excluded Blacks from formal education (in some southern states it was a crime for Blacks to know how to read), the Black press aided the intellectual development of its readers. It may even have served as a primer for Blacks learning how to read. When the *Alienated American* began publishing in Cleveland in 1853, its editor cited education as a major objective. By becoming literate and well informed, wrote the editor, "we can remove every just ground for reproach and faster than ever before, live down the already shallow excuses for our oppression." Almost 100 years later, when the famous Swedish economist Gunnar Myrdal published *An American Dilemma*, his multivolume study of Blacks in America, he singled out the Black press as the most important educational agency for its race.

The Black press served a vital political function. Whether they were fighting for the end to slavery, integration into the political system, or equal economic opportunity, Black editors informed, inspired, unified, and mobilized their readers. They not only offered information; they exhorted their readers to act on this information and told them how to do it. The journals undoubtedly helped Blacks understand, and then realize, their political potential. In fact, some Blacks used journalism as a springboard into politics. Long-time New York City congressman Adam Clayton Powell, Jr. was a journalist (and clergyman) before he served in the House of Representatives. Roy Wilkins was a fiery newspaper columnist before he became the director of the National Association for the Advancement of Colored People.

Wrote one former editor, "The victories in the courts and the exactions from the political parties would have been slower in coming if the Black press were not trumpeting the ills, the dreams and the demands of Black Americans." The famous Black editor T. Thomas Fortune went one step further when he wrote: "A colored newspaper, with 100,000 subscribers, would be a greater power... than any other agency colored man could create... than even fifty Black members of Congress would be." Both Black editors and later historians of the Black press insist that these publications were major contributors to the political progress of the race. Unfortunately, such direct cause-and-effects links are almost impossible to prove.

But certainly it can be said that the Black press, throughout its history, provided one of the most potent arenas in which political, economic, and cultural battles could be fought. Along with the church, the press became a central institution in the Black community. Black editors, as one might suspect, firmly believed this, but so did outside observers. Writing in 1944, Gunnar Myrdal stressed the vital political function of the Black press. "The importance of the Negro press for the formation of Negro opinion... for Negro leadership and concerted action generally is enormous."

THE PRE-CIVIL WAR PRESS

Early Black Writing

The first published writing by Blacks in America predated the appearance of Black newspapers by almost 70 years. In 1760 a Boston man, Briton Hammon, wrote and published his autobiography. The following year, a Long Island, New York slave named Jupiter Hammon (apparently no relation to Briton Hammon) published a series of poems. But perhaps the best-known Black writer during the colonial period was the Boston slave Phillis Wheatley. Educated by her owners, Wheatley was considered a talented poet. Her "An Elegiac Poem on the Death of George Whitefield" published in 1770 was read throughout the colonies. After 1800, a handful of escaped slaves published their autobiographical narratives from northern cities. *The Fugitive Blacksmith*, the autobiography of escaped slave James Pennington, sold out its first edition of 6000 within a year.

Within the cultural context of colonial America, it is astonishing that even these few Black writers were able to work. Enslaved in both the North and the South, considered beasts of burden by white society, excluded from educational institutions, most Blacks had neither the time nor the training to engage in literary pursuits. In many states laws prevented them from undertaking any independent activities. Yet these early writers, working against tremendous odds, set the stage for the emergence of Black publications.

Emergence of Black Journalism

Black journalism, which began with the 1827 publication of *Freedom's Journal*, was almost seven generations behind its white counterpart for obvious reasons. The majority of Blacks in America lived in the South under slavery. Most never left the county they were born in, and few learned to read. With a major part of the potential audience isolated and illiterate, Black journalism was slow to emerge. Not surprisingly, when it did emerge, it surfaced in northern cities and was written by and for ex-slaves and free Black citizens. Of the 38 Black newspapers and magazines published prior to the Civil War, only five were issued from the South. This, in itself, was a feat. Not only was it illegal in some southern states to teach a Black to read, but legal and extralegal interference with the distribution of Black newspapers was the norm in many areas. Nevertheless, New Orleans Blacks published four different journals prior to the Civil War, and Blacks in Augusta, Georgia issued their own newspaper.

But the hub of Black journalism during these years was New York state. Of the 38 newspapers in existence at that time, 19 were published in the state, 11 of them issued from New York City. Although Boston, Philadelphia, Pittsburgh, Cleveland— even San Francisco—were all home to Black publications, New York was the birthplace of Black journalism and its most intense center of activity during the prewar decades. Partly this was because New York had a sizeable population of free Blacks and escaped or freed slaves, but primarily it was a reaction against New York's hostile journalistic and political climate. Boston and

Philadelphia, both of which had significant Black populations, also had strong white Abolitionist societies and white newspapers that were at least not openly hostile to the antislavery cause. A few were even sympathetic. But in New York the Abolitionist movement was not as strong, and several New York City newspapers were vituperous in their attacks against Blacks and white Abolitionists. It was here that two Black freemen, reading vicious attacks on their race, established a journalistic beachhead.

Samuel Cornish, born in Delaware and raised in Philadelphia and New York, was a Presbyterian minister. John B. Russworm, a half-Black Jamaican, was the first Black graduate of a U.S. college. When they read attacks against their race in several of Mordecai M. Noah's New York City newspapers, they were disturbed. When their letters to the editor responding to the attacks were not published, they were outraged. In the spring of 1827 they pooled their resources and began publishing *Freedom's Journal*. Like most of the pre-Civil War newspapers, *Freedom's Journal* was not written for slaves. Cornish and Russworm were freemen, and their newspaper spoke to their free comrades in the North. Of course, the paper was a strong opponent of slavery, but the editors—like most of the pre-Civil War northern Black editors—did not concern themselves with conditions in the South over which they felt they had little direct influence.

The short-lived weekly newspaper had three basic aims: to report the accomplishments of Blacks, to encourage Blacks to strengthen their characters, and to seek "by reason and persuasion" the abolition of slavery. The paper served as a forum for Black protest while at the same time advocating "good manners" among free Blacks as a means to acceptance by white society. Almost immediately, editor Cornish and publisher Russworm found themselves at odds. The issue separating them was the major Black controversy of the decade: colonization. It split Black leaders, Black journalists, and white Abolitionists alike.

The issue was whether Blacks could ever hope to be free and equal participants in white America. Those who believed this was an impossibility, even supposing the end to slavery, advocated sending free Blacks to Africa where they could colonize and create their own society. Russworm was in favor of colonization. But Cornish, in charge of writing and editing the newspaper, was extremely hostile to the plan, and under his editorship *Freedom's Journal* opposed colonization. By the fall of 1827, the rift between the two men had grown so wide that Cornish resigned, returning to the Presbyterian ministry for a time before launching another newspaper. Russworm took over the editorship of the newspaper and the attacks against colonization ceased. Accused by anticolonization Blacks and whites of "selling out," Russworm continued to publish *Freedom's Journal* under heavy attack. Less than a year later, following his own advice, he settled in Liberia where he became the superintendent of public schools and later the editor of the Liberia *Herald*. He went on to have a successful political career in Liberia, becoming the governor of a colony at Cape Palmas.

Freedom's Journal was dead, but Samuel Cornish's career as a Black editor was not finished. A year after quitting over the colonization controversy, Cornish started another newspaper, *Rights for All*. Although the newspaper failed to gather sufficient support and died within two years, Cornish had established another forum for his anticolonization ideas. Undaunted, he began publishing a third newspaper, the *Weekly Advocate*, in 1837. "The Advocate," he wrote in the prospectus for the New York paper, "will be like a chain, binding you together as one." Echoing his plea of a decade earlier when he began *Freedom's Journal*, Cornish wrote: "O how often we have been degraded and insulted, and how frequently do we feel the want of an ADVOCATE among us!"

But within a year, the *Advocate* had been replaced by Cornish's fourth journalistic effort, *The Colored American*. Backed by two Black men, Cornish finally edited what can be considered the first successful Black newspaper. Publishing continuously for five years, *The Colored American* reached 2,000 subscribers in the towns of northern states from Maine to Michigan. The object of the new paper, wrote Cornish, was "the moral, social and political elevation and improvement of the free colored people; and the peaceful emancipation of the enslaved." The New York paper was, of course, a strident opponent of colonization. Beyond that, it served as a local bulletin for New York City Blacks and a chronicler of the activities of northern Blacks in the state and national antislavery movement and in the moral, educational, and cultural societies of the day.

The names of the publications during the first few decades of Black journalism reveal their antislavery aims: *Mirror of Libery, Palladium of Liberty, Genius of Freedom, Herald of Freedom,*

Freedman's Advocate, The Elevator. But although these papers were united in their goal to end slavery, it would be a mistake to look at the early Black press as monolithic. The publications were as rich with controversy as the times. The colonization dispute, which began when the American Colonization society, a white organization, was founded in 1817, continued through the 1850s. Another enduring controversy was exclusivism. Should Blacks create their own Abolition societies, their own churches, their own schools, or should they strive for inclusion within the white institutions? Both white Abolitionists and Black leaders were split on the issue.

The *National Reformer*, a Black magazine published in Philadelphia by the American Moral Reform Society, called for the elimination of racial distinction within institutions. Blacks and whites should fight together for the emancipation of slaves, wrote the editors in 1838. But Samuel Cornish's *The Colored American* disagreed. The results of certain projects would be more discernible if Blacks worked by themselves to achieve their goals, wrote Cornish in 1838. Both separate and integrated Abolition societies existed in the pre-Civil War period, some Black leaders wrote for both Black and white publications, and a few white sympathizers financially supported Black publications. The controversy was never settled.

The 1840s began auspiciously for Black journalism with the publication of *Ram's Horn* in 1841. When Willis Hodges was forced to pay $15 to see his antislavery letter published in the New York *Sun*, he resolved to start a publication of his own. "I had not a dollar of my own for the paper," Hodges later wrote,

> but as white washing was good business in New York, I went to work at it, and in two months I had nearly all the money that was necessary to get out the first number; and I can truly say that I furnished every dollar that started the Ram's Horn.

The weekly paper, which published for seven years and attracted a peak of 2,500 subscribers, was noted for its articles by Frederick Douglass and John Brown.

Almost all Black publications of the era began this way. Although a few—notably the early Black magazines—were backed by church groups or moral improvement societies, most publications had only the backing of their usually impoverished editor and founder. Sometimes subscriptions kept the publication afloat, but more often the editor-publisher supported his journalistic enterprise by engaging in other work. *The Elevator*, which began publication in Albany, New York in 1842, was an exception. The antislavery weekly was backed by a group of sympathetic white New York editors and their Abolitionist friends. Horace Greeley, who had founded the New York *Tribune* the year before, Henry J. Raymond, Greeley's chief assistant and later the founder of the New York *Times*, Thurlow Weed, a powerful Albany editor, and several white Abolitionists supplied the money for the undertaking.

Frederick Douglass

The most important Black newspaper of the 1840s—perhaps the most important Black newspaper of the pre-Civil War period—was Frederick Douglass' *North Star*. Douglass had fled to New England after escaping slavery in 1838. In the early 1840s he contributed columns to two New York-based weeklies, *The National Slavery Standard* and *Ram's Horn*, and lectured for the American Anti-Slavery Society. In 1845 he traveled to England, where Abolitionist friends raised enough money to buy his freedom from his Maryland owner and to donate a little more than $2,000 toward the publication of a new newspaper.

Unlike most of his journalistic predecessors, Douglass did not begin publishing *North Star* because he was refused access to other forums. As the leading Black Abolitionist of his time, Douglass easily could have contributed to the white Abolitionist journals. In fact, his white Abolitionist friends tried to discourage him from beginning the new venture. The existing Abolitionist press was sufficient, they said. Previous efforts by Black journalists had been short-lived, and if a well-known leader like Douglass were to fail, the white Abolitionists believed the damage to the movement would be irreparable.

But Douglass was searching for more than a personal forum for his antislavery writings. He wanted to create a successful Black newspaper to prove to both whites and Blacks that Black journalism was not inferior. He began publication on November 1, 1847 and issued either a weekly or a monthly newspaper for the next 16 years. The *North Star* attacked slavery, advocated universal emancipation, and called for the moral and intellectual improvement of the race. It was filled with contributions from correspondents in Europe, the West Indies, and throughout the United States. With a subscription list of 3,000, it was the first Black paper to have considerable circulation among non-Black Americans. Because of its eloquence, its duration, and its following, the *North Star* is considered the high point of Black journalism in the pre-Civil War era.

But Douglass was not immune to the problems that faced other Black editors. The people of Rochester, New York, home of the *North Star*, were antagonistic. Douglass's house mysteriously caught fire and 12 volumes of his paper were destroyed. At one point, the New York *Herald* wrote: "The editor should be exiled to Canada and his presses thrown into the lake." The major problem, however, was money. Douglass couldn't cover the cost of the paper by subscriptions, and advertising in Black journals was almost unheard of. He was forced to spend a great deal of time on the lecture circuit to subsidize the paper. In 1851 he merged *North Star* with another newspaper, hoping to reduce expenses and widen his audience. The new paper, *Frederick Douglass' Paper*, continued through the 1850s. In the early 1860s, finding the financial struggle of weekly journalism too great, Douglass started *Douglass' Monthly* which continued publication until 1863.

The Press and Controversy

Throughout the 1840s and 1850s, Douglass and his journalistic colleagues were engaged in two more controversies that split the Black press. The first involved Blacks' support of the U.S. government. Most Black leaders and editors pledged loyalty to the Constitution and limited their arguments to which political party to support. But some, including Douglass, agreed with the great Abolitionist William Lloyd Garrison when he said that the Constitution was "an agreement with Hell." These Garrisonian Abolitionists asked, "Why support the Constitution when it excludes Blacks from the political life of the nation?" At a meeting of the American Anti-Slavery Society, Douglass said:

> I have no patriotism. I have no country. . . . I cannot have any love for this country or for its Constitution. I desire to see its overthrow as speedily as possible and its Constitution slivered in a thousand fragments.

But by the early 1850s, Douglass had formally and publicly changed his mind, joining the ranks of those who supported the Constitution. Other Black leaders and editors, however, continued to suggest ignoring the Constitution and engaging in civil disobedience.

The second controversy—one that had been brewing for 20 years—involved the use of violence to achieve Black freedom. Although most Black leaders and editors preached nonviolence, particularly in the 1830s and 1840s, a significant and vocal minority called for militant action. In 1829 David Walker, who had been a Boston agent for *Freedom's Journal*, published a pamphlet calling for the death of slaveowners. "Are they not the Lord's enemies?" he asked. "Ought they not be destroyed?"

Walker's *Appeal* was unequaled in intensity until Rev. Henry Highland Garnet's 1843 "Address to the Slaves of the United States of America" in which he exhorted slaves to "arise . . . strike for your lives and liberties." Late in the 1840s, Douglass joined the fray when he wrote, in *North Star:*

> if the slave should put [the slave owners] to the sword tomorrow, who dare say that the criminals deserved less than death at the hands of their long-abused chattels?

When the Fugitive Slave Law was enacted in 1850 (a master could, merely by filing a claim, seize runaway slaves without granting them the right to a jury trial), an increasing number of Black editors and leaders called for militancy. When the Supreme Court declared that Congress had no power to prevent slavery in the territories—the Dred Scott decision of 1859—the militancy versus restraint issue intensified. While some editors continued to counsel restraint, Douglass became even more militant. "What we want is anti-slavery government," he wrote in 1859. "For this the ballot is needed, and if this will not be heard or heeded, then the bullet."

It was the bullet. From 1861 to 1865 North battled South and the future of American Blacks hung in the balance. It had always been difficult for Black journalism to exist in the South; now it was impossible. In the North some Black newspapers and magazines ceased publication, and few new ventures were started. Apparently the conventional white media in the North, along with the white Abolitionist press, provided enough of an outlet for antislavery sentiments. The Black papers that did continue publishing throughout the war were understandably militant. The (San Francisco) *Pacific Appeal*, the only Black newspaper west of the Rockies, urged Blacks to join the fight. "He who would be free himself must strike the first blow" was the newspaper's motto in 1862. Frederick Douglass was more explicit. In the early years of the war he used *Douglass' Monthly* to urge for the inclusion of Blacks in the military. "We are fighting them with only one hand when we should be fighting them with both," he wrote in February of 1862. "[Why are we] striking the rebels with our soft white hand when we should be striking with the iron hand of the Black man?" Douglass ceased publishing his monthly newspaper in August 1863, writing that he felt his services were needed in organizing Black troops. He had received a commission in the northern army.

THE POST-CIVIL WAR
NINETEENTH-CENTURY PRESS

By the end of the Civil war, only 24 Black journals were still being published. But immediately after the war, Black journalism began to flourish. From April 1865 to January 1866, a dozen new publications started, half of them in the South. From 1865 to 1875, Black newspapers appeared in eight states that had previously had no Black journals. By 1880, Black newspapers were being published in 19 states, including eight states in the deep South, and 15 Black magazines were started. By 1890, 29 states were home to more than 150 Black newspapers. Twenty-eight magazines got their start during the decade. In all, almost 1,200 new Black newspapers and magazines were born from 1865 to 1900.

The spread of Black journalism in the decades after the Civil War is easy to understand. In the South, freed slaves, now able to earn money to buy newspapers, were anxious to read about themselves and their compatriots. The war had widened their world view. Now that Black men could vote (Black women would have to wait for the franchise, along with their white sisters, until 1920), there were compelling reasons for them to read and learn about politics and government. The Black social service and "improvement" societies that sprang up throughout the South often published their own journals and sometimes lent financial assistance to other newspapers and magazines. In the aftermath of the war, many Blacks migrated northward. Concentrating in racially homogeneous communities, they were now capable of supporting new journalistic efforts.

Conservatism and Reconstruction

Reconstruction-era and late nineteenth-century Black journals were both numerous and diverse. But they were less militant and perhaps less influential than their pre-Civil War predecessors. In the early years of Reconstruction, the Black press urged a policy of reconciliation and cooperation in rebuilding the country. Wrote the editor of the Charleston, South Carolina *Advocate* in 1867: "In the great works of Reconstruction, we should scorn the idea of a white or black man's party. . . . We should all live together in peace and harmony." The Augusta, Georgia *Colored American* proclaimed itself "devoted to the promotion of harmony and good will between white and colored people of the South." Reflecting the cautious optimism of the time, most Black publications supported Reconstruction efforts and did not speak out for additional rights.

Many papers concentrated on education as a means of self-elevation, printing information on farming, business practices, and household management. Other papers allied themselves with the Republican Party and attempted to influence voting behavior. Politicians became editors and editors became office-seekers. A smattering of newspapers and magazines turned their attention to cultural rather than political matters. The San Francisco *Elevator* focused on art, science, literature, and drama. In Georgia, the *Colored American* aimed to be "a vehicle for the diffusion of religious, political and general intelligence." In New York T. Thomas Fortune began publishing *Rumour*, a sophisticated 12-page weekly aimed at the Black intelligentsia. The paper, which later became the New York *Globe*, emphasized racial issues but also published poetry and literature. Woodcuts of famous Blacks were reproduced on the front page.

In the decades following the Civil War, most Black editors urged internal unity and loyalty to the Republican Party. But the press, as in years past, was not monolithic. H. C. Smith, editor of the Cleveland *Gazette*, was a leader of Black democrats.

T. Thomas Fortune consistently urged independent political action in his newspaper. And a handful of Black editors and leaders flirted with various third-party efforts, including the Populist or People's Party, which found a growing constituency in the South during the 1870s and 1880s. But the majority of Black editors continued to support the party of Lincoln, even after it was clear that Reconstruction efforts in the South were not achieving racial equality.

A number of southern Blacks, realizing that Reconstruction may have actually worsened their condition, fled westward. In the late 1870s, Blacks established colonies across the Mississippi, and in 1879 the great Black exodus to Kansas began. Newspapers were not far behind the new immigrants. Within a few years, Topeka was home to three Black newspapers, and smaller towns—including the all-Black settlement of Nicodemus—sprouted Black journals. Although a few of these publications continued to crusade for equality, most, like those in the East and South, saw education as their main mission.

One major exception to the apolitical nature of the late nineteenth-century Black press was the Baltimore *Afro-American*. Founded in 1892 by John H. Murphy and his son, Dr. Carl Murphy, both of whom were key figures in Maryland politics, the *Afro-American* tackled a variety of controversial issues. The paper financed the first lawsuit contesting Southern Railroad's "Jim Crow" trains that ran south from Washington, D.C. The Murphys attacked the Maryland Art Institute and University of Maryland Law School for not admitting Black students, and their paper initiated the fight to equalize Black and white teachers' salaries in the state. The *Afro-American*, like its prewar ancestors, was a fighting newspaper.

At the same time, women began to make inroads into the Black press. While their white counterparts had limited roles in the conventional press—often working one to a paper and allowed to cover only fashion and society news—Black women were editing their own newspapers and contributing columns to many of the major urban papers. Weekly newspapers in Iowa, Alabama, Virginia, Michigan, and Maryland were owned and edited by Black women during the 1880s and 1890s. Ida B. Wells-Barnett of Mississippi, perhaps the best known of these early Black women journalists, was half-owner and editor of the Mississippi *Free Speech* until the newspaper's plant was sacked in 1892. Moving to Chicago in the mid-1890s, she continued to write for both Black and white publications. Dozens of women contributed to other newspapers and magazines on subjects ranging from scientific discoveries to music. A few edited temperance columns within established weeklies, and women held all the editorial positions on several church-related publications.

After a little more than 60 years, 30 of them during the most adverse of times, the Black press was well established. Although continually troubled by financial woes—lack of advertising and small circulation—the press had become an important part of Black society. But in all those years, Black journalists had never produced a daily newspaper. The costs were high and the risks great. It took a financially secure, successful printer in Cairo, Illinois to pioneer the daily press. W. S. Scott, whose printing office did all of the city's job printing, had been publishing a weekly paper. In 1882 he transformed the Cairo *Gazette* into the *Daily Gazette*. With a sizable circulation among the white community, the *Gazette* lasted for six months until Scott's shop was destroyed by fire. Five years later, the Columbus, Georgia *Messenger*, first published as a weekly, entered the daily field. But after a financially troubled year and a half, the paper reverted to weekly publication. With few exceptions, the Black press remained a weekly phenomenon. In the late nineteenth and early twentieth centuries, lack of advertising revenue prevented the daily press from succeeding. In later years, as more Blacks moved into the middle class and were perceived by whites as viable targets for advertising, the well-established, large-circulation white daily press provided too much competition for the fledgling Black dailies.

The Conciliation Controversy

Toward the end of the nineteenth century and into the first decade of the twentieth century, three men dominated Black journalism. Booker T. Washington, William Monroe Trotter and W.E.B. DuBois—all prominent spokesmen as well as journalists and editors—were the key figures in a major controversy that rocked the Black community: Should Blacks agitate for equality or should they accept segregation and subservience to whites (so-called conciliation)? To different degrees Trotter and DuBois believed in agitation. Washington called for conciliation.

Booker T. Washington was a relatively obscure principal of a relatively obscure Black training school, Tuskegee Institute, until September 18, 1895. On that day he delivered a speech at Georgia's state exposition calling for Blacks to put aside their quest for social and political equality. "The wisest among my race," he told his not surprisingly enthusiastic white audience, "understand that the agitation of questions of social equality is to extreme folly." Washington's views might have remained just that had he not successfully employed a spate of Black newspapers including the powerful New York *Age* to expound on conciliation. His manipulation of the Black press, perhaps more than his opinions, angered the prominent Black spokesmen of his time.

Washington not only found various forums for his ideas, but he managed to silence many of his journalistic critics by buying out or subsidizing important Black newspapers. Money from white philanthropists, understandably fond of Washington's views, helped him purchase Black newspapers or provide sufficient financial banking so that he was able to influence editorial content. From 1895 to 1915 Washington so dominated Black journalism that opponents of conciliation had to start their own newspapers if they wanted to mount a sustained attack on his view.

William Monroe Trotter did just that. Raised in comfortable circumstances in Boston, elected to Phi Beta Kappa at Harvard, Trotter founded the Boston *Guardian* in 1901. His object was to counter the hegemony of Washington's conciliatory rhetoric by disseminating his own pro-agitation views in his own newspaper. Until W.E.B. DuBois came on the scene four years later, Trotter's was the only paper of any longevity providing an outlet for anti-Washington views. But the absence of Black journalism challenging Washington did not mean the Black community endorsed conciliation.

When Washington spoke on conciliation in Boston in 1903, Trotter, who was in the audience, tried to question him. When the authorities arrested Trotter for disrupting the speech, fistfights broke out in the auditorium. A clergyman who was also in attendance later wrote:

The revolt at Boston was the first that has reached the public. There would be others if Mr. Washington did not control the strong papers conducted by colored men and if they expressed the sentiments of the people.

W.E.B. DuBois read Trotter's *Guardian* and approved of its militancy, particularly on the issues of Black education and voting. A writer, teacher, and journalist, DuBois devoted his life to challenging the concepts of white supremacy and Black inferiority. He objected not only to Washington's views but to his method of buying up the Black press and attempting to close off even mild and reasonable opposition. In 1905, DuBois introduced the first of the five periodicals he was to publish in the service of Black equality. The *Moon Illustrated Weekly* lasted less than a year and reached only 300 subscribers in Memphis and Atlanta, but it provided DuBois with a personal forum. It was the first attempt at a national Black magazine and the beginning of DuBois' journalistic career. From 1907 to 1910, he published *The Horizon* from Washington, D.C., using the monthly magazine to attack conciliation and promote an unfettered and unsubsidized Black press. The publication also included book reviews, poems, short stories, and articles about prominent Blacks. In 1910 he began his 24-year association with *The Crisis*, the official journal of the National Association for the Advancement of Colored People. Here he presented his most cogent arguments for racial quality. *The Crisis*, which began with a press run of 500, reached a peak circulation of 100,000 by 1918. DuBois also founded a Black children's magazine, *The Brownies Book*, and *Phylon*, a scholarly journal on world race problems published at Atlanta University.

THE PRESS IN THE FIRST HALF
OF THE TWENTIETH CENTURY

When Booker T. Washington died in 1915, the conciliation controversy died with him. The Black press, bolstered by the arrival of large-circulation newspapers in the eastern and midwestern urban centers, ceased its infighting and began to concentrate on attacking white discrimination. One of the most interesting and historically significant Black papers founded before World War I was Robert S. Abbott's Chicago *Defender*.

When Abbott, an ex-southerner who worked as a printer, founded the *Defender* in 1905, he said he had the following assets: a card table, a borrowed chair, and 25 cents. The first two issues were published on credit. But within ten years, the *Defender* had more than 200,000 subscribers in both the North and the South. Abbott's editor, J. Hockley Smiley, performed the miracle. Applying the popular muckraking style of journalism to Black issues, Smiley created dramatic editorial content. Crime, scandal, race riots, lynchings, and activities of the Ku Klux Klan filled the pages of the *Defender*. In fact, the paper established the tradition of exposé journalism in the Black press. It also promoted the northward migration of Blacks, and to help make the transition from South to North a smoother one, it published train schedules, job opportunities, and housing information.

Abbott, while appealing to the Black urban mass audience he and the southern depression of 1914 helped create, revolutionized Black journalism in the process. He created a press for the masses, not the educated elite. The *Defender* was not only a pioneer of its time, it also had special significance to Black journalism later in the twentieth century. After Abbott's death in 1940, his nephew John Sengstacke took over as publisher and made the *Defender* the cornerstone of the largest Black newspaper group in America.

World War I and the Fight Against Discrimination

When the United States declared war on Germany in April 1917, the Black press reacted less than enthusiastically. To many Black leaders and editors who saw racial inequality and discrimination at home, "make the world safe for democracy" was a hollow war cry. Blacks in America had yet to enjoy the fruits of democracy. Domestic events reinforced this feeling. In 1917, 35 Blacks were lynched in the South, and East St. Louis was rocked by bloody race riots. Some Blacks, like this writer from the Richmond, Virigina *Planet*, refused to support the war effort:

> Unless I am assured that the flag will offer protection to the 12,000,000 colored people in the country, and unless I am convinced that world democracy includes Black men as well as white men, I shall consider myself a disgrace to my race and country by freely volunteering to fight for democracy across the seas, because I firmly believe and maintain that democracy, like charity, should begin at home.

That issue of the *Planet* was declared unmailable under the provisions of the 1917 Espionage Act that made it a crime to utter "disloyal or abusive language" about the government.

They may have had serious doubts about whether the war abroad would help democracy at home, but almost all Black editors supported the war. Some felt that nonsupport, however justified, would harm the Black cause irreparably. Others believed Black participation in the war could be a way of showcasing Black equality. But support of the war did not mean an end to domestic criticism in the Black press.

The Chicago *Defender*, perhaps the most militant Black paper during World War I, relentlessly attacked the discrimination and segregation of Black troops. The paper's cartoonist, Leslie Rogers, drew a picture of Black troops facing Germans as the Blacks were being shot in the back by white troops. Abbott was almost jailed for this under the Espionage Act. He avoided imprisonment by purchasing a number of liberty bonds and agreeing to encourage bond purchase in his newspaper. Editors of the other powerful Black newspapers—New York *Age*, Boston *Guardian*, Baltimore *Afro-American*, and Cleveland *Gazette*—joined the *Defender* in decrying segregation in the military.

When World War I began, there were no officer training facilities for Blacks. DuBois made this his special crusade. In the pages of *The Crisis*, he urged the government to create officers' training camps "to prevent the spread of disloyalty and resentment among the Black masses." But DuBois, to the horror of Abbott and many of the other leading Black editors, proposed segregated training camps. He saw segregation as a necessary evil. DuBois' editorials led to the founding of the Central Committee of Negro College Men at Howard University, a group of 1,500 Black college graduates ready to volunteer for officers' training. Later the government created Ft. Des Moines, an all-Black training facility for officers. But this did little to curb criticism within the Black press.

The attacks by Black papers on discrimination in the armed forces were perceived as so threatening that George Creel's Committee on Public Information (a war propaganda agency) sent out circulars proclaiming that enemy agents were the cause of Blacks' dissatisfaction. "German agents have thousands of propagandists among the Negroes, exciting them with stories of impossible atrocities committed against the colored people,"

read the circular. In 1919, the Justice Department accused
Russian interests of supplying funds for propaganda to stir up
race antagonism in the United States. J. Edgar Hoover, the
compiler of the case, never made public any evidence to
support these allegations.

Black editors knew, of course, that no foreign agents were
behind their criticisms of discrimination within the U.S. military,
but they felt they had to react publicly and decisively to the
accusation. In June 1918, at a special conference, 31 Black
editors adopted resolutions reaffirming that the struggle against
Germany was paramount and pledging the loyalty of the Black
people. They resolved to "use our every endeavor to keep all of
these 12,000,000 people at the highest pitch, not simply of
passive loyalty, but of active and self-sacrificing participation."
In fact, more than 350,000 Blacks served in the military during
World War I.

Between the Wars

But when Blacks returned from active duty, they returned to
race riots and intense discrimination. In the summer of 1919 six
people were killed and 150 injured during a Washington, D.C.
riot. In Chicago 23 Blacks were killed and 537 people injured.
There were 26 race riots that summer. The following year, the
Mississippi state legislature made it a misdemeanor to print or
publish "appeals, arguments or suggestions favoring social
equality between the white and black races." One city in
Tennessee passed an ordinance against the circulation of Black
newspapers. The lynchings continued. Perhaps as a reaction to
the deteriorating domestic scene, Marcus Garvey's "Back to
Africa" movement achieved postwar popularity.

Marcus Manasseh Garvey, sometimes called The Black
Moses, edited and published eight journals, inspired at least
three others, and established the first Black book publishing
company. In all his endeavors, including a short-lived daily in
New York, *Negro Times*, Garvey preached Black nationalism
and the return to Africa. Only by returning to their ancestral land
could Blacks ever achieve equality and live in social harmony,
Garvey believed. One of his papers, a New York weekly called
Negro World, had more than 200,000 subscribers worldwide.

But most Black editors continued to crusade for equality within U.S. society during the period between the two world wars. *The Crisis*, the *Guardian*, the *Defender*, and hundreds of other Black newspapers and magazines relentlessly exposed discrimination and opposed violence against Blacks. *The Negro Yearbook* reported that at least 21 new Black newspapers were started in the decade after World War I. The Depression hurt the Black press, as it hurt many other businesses. In the 1930s, close to 80 Black journals ceased publication. But the period also saw the birth of 32 new newspapers and an overall increase in circulation. In 1940, the U.S. Department of Commerce reported that circulation of Black newspapers exceeded 1.25 million. Clearly Black Americans still felt they needed a press of their own and were willing to support it. Still, most newspapers and magazines subsisted on single-copy sales, included only advertising of Black businesses or Black-oriented products, and attracted no national advertising.

World War II and the Double V Campaign

In 1940 Black editors met in Chicago to try to remedy the advertising problem. They established the National Negro Publishing Association, with the *Defender's* John Sengstacke as president, as an advertising recruitment agency. Looking to the war in Europe and remembering government criticism of the World War I Black press, the editors pledged full support for Roosevelt's war policies and loyalty to the United States. But during World War II, although the Black press supported the war effort, it continued to criticize racism both at home and in the military.

Black journalism was a force to be reckoned with during the war years. Black papers were being published in 32 states, and national Black weeklies in Pittsburgh, Chicago, Baltimore, and Norfolk (Virginia) were reaching hundreds of thousands of Black Americans throughout the nation. Although the circulation of Black journals in 1943 was a little more than 1.5 million, the readership probably exceeded 5 million. The weekly newspapers and monthly magazines stayed in the home longer than dailies, circulating among friends and neighbors. One observer estimated that half of America's 13 million Blacks read a Black newspaper every week during the war years.

What they read in these newspapers was news they could not get elsewhere: features about Blacks in the armed forces (700,000 served during the war) and exposés of the problems facing Black service personnel. Black journals reported on discrimination within the military and, after 1941, called for the end to the racial quota system and segregation in the armed forces. Reporters for the *Afro-American* and *Defender* wrote critical stories on the conditions of Blacks in army training camps. The Red Cross, which would not accept blood from Blacks, also came under fire. As in 1917, editors were attacked for undermining the war effort with their exposés.

Black editors mounted what they called the "Double V Campaign"—victory over racism at home and victory over Nazism in Europe. Echoing Black journalism of the World War I era, the editors maintained that fighting racism abroad while supporting it at home was hyprocrisy. Their definition of racism went beyond their own race. Black papers decried the internment of Japanese-Americans after Pearl Harbor. Suppose the United States and Liberia were someday at war, editorialized the Chicago *Defender*. Would Black Americans be herded into detention camps?

In addition to calling their readers' attention to continued domestic inequality and racism within the military, Black editors sent their own correspondents overseas to cover the war. More than 30 Black war reporters throughout Europe and the Far East sent back dispatches to their home newspapers, informing readers of the efforts of Black military personnel. Newspapers built prestige with their war reportage and attracted talented Black journalists. By the end of the war, the paid weekly circulation of the Black press exceeded 2 million.

THE MODERN BLACK PRESS

But the postwar years brought a decline in both the circulation and influence of the well-established newspapers. Television, which affected readership of the white press as well, took its toll. The early civil rights movement forced the white press to pay at least some attention to Black issues, thus creating competition for Black readers. At the same time, the white press slowly began to open its doors to Black reporters. With higher salaries and greater prestige in the offing, some talented Black journalists left the Black press for careers in the white media. As more Blacks began to move into the middle class, they left behind both the inner city and the newspapers that served the Black urban population. Additionally, Black newspapers and magazines continued to be weakened by lack of advertising support. Although publication of the book, *The $30 Billion Negro*, heightened white awareness of Blacks as consumers, as late as the 1970s, all Black media combined received less than 1% of advertising agency billings.

The story of Black journalism in the second half of the twentieth century is, for the most part, the story of political moderatism and corporate growth. The white press had long had its empire builders—men like Hearst and Scripps, and later corporations like Gannett and Newhouse—who owned and controlled chains of newspapers. By the mid-twentieth century, Black journalism had its empire builders too. The Murphy family, owners of the Baltimore *Afro-American*, started a chain of *Afro-Americans*. The Scott family, publishers of the Atlanta *World*, increased its holdings in the South. John Sengstacke, who had inherited the Chicago *Defender* from his uncle Robert S. Abbott, bought newspapers in Pennsylvania, Ohio, Michigan, Georgia, Florida, Louisiana, and Tennessee. John H. Johnson started a magazine empire that grew to include *Ebony, Ebony International, Jet, Black World, Hue*, and several other publications. The Good Publishing Company of Ft. Worth, Texas published four magazines, and Tuesday Publications, Inc. produced a 2 million circulation Black magazine supplement inserted into both Black and white newspapers. In most cases, Black newspapers and magazines abandoned political controversy in their quest for advertising dollars.

But controversy and radicalism did not disappear entirely from Black journalism during the 1960s and 1970s. *Mr. Muhammed Speaks to the Blackman*, first published in Harlem in 1960 and then moved to Chicago with the shortened name *Muhammed Speaks*, was a forum for the militant leader Malcolm X. By the early 1970s, the newspaper had a circulation of 500,000. The second-highest-circulation Black newspaper of the decade was the outspoken *Black Panther*, a weekly published in Oakland, California. Founded in 1967 by Black Panther party leaders Huey Newton and Bobby Seale, the paper decried police treatment of Blacks and called for various programs for Black self-determination. It reached a peak circulation of 200,000 in the early 1970s.

Throughout the 1960s and 1970s, Blacks attempted to establish their own news services, not to compete with the white wire services like Associated Press but to gather and disseminate news concerning Black Americans. In 1970, the Community News Service, funded by a Ford Foundation grant, established news bureaus in Harlem, Brooklyn, and the South Bronx for the purpose of improving white media coverage of minority news. For six years, the service delivered daily bulletins to CBS, NBC, the New York *Times*, and other subscribers. In 1972, two Black news services based in Washington, D.C. began sending subscriber papers national and international news pertaining to Blacks. Also in the 1970s, three Black radio news services were established to disseminate news to the more than 180 radio stations that were partially or totally Black oriented. (Of those, fewer than 4% were Black-owned.)

By the mid-1970s, more than 200 Black weekly newspapers were reaching 4.3 million readers. Five dailies and approximately 175 magazines were serving Black Americans. But observers of Black journalism were not happy. They criticized the Black press for its middle-class orientation, saying the press had limited value for the millions of Blacks still living in urban ghettos. They decried the moderate stance of most Black publications. Detroit mayor Coleman Young told Black editors in 1974:

> I think there has been a tendency on the part of Black papers to look to the advertising too much and forget that power rests with the people. We must have a militant press . . . one that takes a position.

Although some Black leaders are unhappy with the current direction of the Black press, and although the press itself shrank to fewer than 100 weeklies and only one daily in 1980, it is clear that Black journalism still serves an important function in American society. Some newspapers continue to attack racism, school segregation, the lack of equal opportunity, and conditions of urban ghetto life. Even the moderate Black press, which shies away from controversy, provides its Black readers with news about themselves. The white media, with few exceptions, continue to ignore the diverse achievements—and the serious problems—of 10% of the population.

"We need a press of our own," wrote a Black editor in the 1850s. It is no less true in the 1980s.

REFERENCES

The following material aided in the preparation of this chapter and is suggested for further reading:

Bryan, Carter R. "Negro Journalism in American Before Emancipation." *Journalism Monographs*, 12 (September 1969).

Bullock, Penelope. *The Afro-American Periodical Press, 1938-1909*. Baton Rouge: Louisiana State University Press, 1981.

Burns, W. Haywood. *The Voices of Negro Protest in America*. London: Oxford University Press, 1963.

Dann, Martin E. *The Black Press 1827-1890: The Quest for National Unity*. New York: G. P. Putnam's Sons, 1971.

Detweiler, Frederick G. *The Negro Press in the United States*. Chicago: University of Chicago Press, 1922.

Dick, Robert C. *Black Protest: Issues and Tactics*. Westport, CT: Greenwood Press, 1974.

Douglass, Frederick. *Life and Times of Frederick Douglass*. Hartford, CT: Park Publishing, 1882.

DuBois, W.E.B. *The Autobiography of W.E.B. DuBois,* ed. by Herbert Aptheker. New York: International Publishing, 1968.

Filler, Louis. *The Crusade Against Slavery, 1830-1860*. New York: Harper & Brothers, 1960.

Finkle, Lee. *Forum for Protest: The Black Press during World War II*. Canbury, NJ: Associated University Presses, 1975.

Fleming, James G. "108 Years of the Negro Press." *Opportunity*, XII (March 1935), p. 75.

Gore, George W. Jr. *Negro Journalism*. Greencastle, IN: Journalism Press, 1922.

LaBrie, Henry G., ed. *Perspectives of the Black Press, 1974*. Kennebunkport, ME: Mercer House Press, 1974.

Myrdal, Gunnar. *An American Dilemma: The Negro Problem and Modern Democracy*. New York: Harper & Brothers, 1944.

Oak, Vishnu V. *The Negro Newspaper*. Yellow Springs, OH: Antioch Press, 1948.

Penn, I. Garland. *The Afro-American Press and Its Editors,* reprint of the 1891 edition. New York: Arno Press and the New York Times, 1969.

Pride, Armistead. "Negro Newspapers: Yesterday, Today and Tomorrow." *Journalism Quarterly*, 28 (Spring 1951), pp. 179-188.

Quarles, Benjamin. *Black Abolitionists*. New York: Oxford University Press, 1969.

Tinney, James S. and Rector, Justine, eds. *Issues and Trends in Afro-American Journalism*. Lanham, MD: University Press of America, 1980.

Wolseley, Roland E. *The Black Press, U.S.A.* Ames: Iowa State University Press, 1971.

3

SEEKERS OF A NEW AGE

A map of the world that does not include Utopia is not even worth glancing at.

—Oscar Wilde

When sixteenth-century English statesman and author Sir Thomas More created the imaginary island of Utopia, he gave a name to the fundamental human yearning for harmony, peace, and perfection. Utopia, where political and legal systems functioned flawlessly, where social and moral ideals were reality, and where strife was nonexistent, was heaven on earth. More's Utopia existed only in the pages of his book, but throughout history and throughout the world countless men and women have created living utopias, working models of what they believed to be perfect societies. But perhaps nowhere has the idea of utopia been so much a part of the national consciousness as in America.

Long before America was discovered, Europeans imagined a utopia to the west. It was a land of innocence, a land of plenty, a paradise. To the Puritans, America's first European settlers, the New World was a pristine wilderness selected by God as the site for a devout settlement of Protestant dissidents. Setting out to establish an ideal society based on their interpretation of the word of God, the Puritans were, in effect, America's first utopians. They began what was to become a tradition of American experimentation. For the next three and a half centuries, diverse visions of perfect societies motivated Americans of various religious, political, and cultural ideals to create hundreds of utopian colonies. "The impulse to experiment . . . and to challenge orthodox patterns is deeply engrained in our social history," writes Robert Fogerty, a historian of utopias.

United by both their ideals and their desire to live them, utopian colonists believed they had found the solution to the problems of their day. Naturally, they wanted to spread the word. But their ideas—from collective ownership of property to anarchy, from "free love" to celibacy—were threatening to mainstream society. Their colonies were often tiny, geographically isolated enclaves that lasted only a few years. Given this, their access to the mainstream press of their day was minimal at best. Although one or two of the most famous colonies were covered by sympathetic editors, most of the conventional press, like the society it mirrored, ignored or ridiculed the utopians. Colonists who wanted to inform, educate, propagandize, and recruit found it necessary to start their own newspapers and periodicals.

UTOPIANISM IN AMERICA

Although utopian colonies have taken as many forms as there have been visions and ideals of perfect societies, they do share some fundamental similarities. The experiments were responses to what colonists perceived as the evils of their day, be they religious, moral, ethical, political, economic, or social. Attracting a wide variety of malcontents and "seekers,'" the colonies generally strived for self-sufficiency, self-development, social brotherhood, freedom, and equality. Some had religious and spiritual goals. Others were organized for economic and social purposes. Still others were based on political ideals. But most fell into two basic categories: outer-directed, political (in its largest sense), leaderless experiments and inner-directed, apolitical, disciplined experiments.

The first utopian experiments in America were of the latter type and were religious in nature. Puritans were soon followed by other small religious sects who, feeling persecuted in their European homelands, came to America to establish communal enclaves. The Dutch Mennonites, the German and Scandinavian Quakers, the Moravians, and the Rappites all founded settlements bound by both religious tenets and communal and cooperative practices. Beginning in the Revolutionary War era, the Shakers, a religious sect that lived communally and observed celibacy, established colonies. In the first half of the

nineteenth century, the Mormons, a religious sect with communal and polygamous practices, moved from New York to
Ohio, then Illinois, and finally Utah in search of religious
freedom.

In the early and mid-1800s, outer-directed, socially and
politically conscious utopian experiments proliferated. Robert
Owen, a Welsh socialist and philanthropist who believed a
person's character was wholly determined by environment,
founded several Owenite communities in the 1820s, including
one in New Harmony, Indiana. Followers of Charles Fourier, a
French social scientist and reformer, established dozens of
colonies throughout the Northeast and Midwest during the
1840s and 1850s. Social equality, collective labor, and self-
sufficiency were the hallmarks of Fourierist experiments like
Brook Farm, Hopedale, Fruitlands, and Icaria. At the same time,
John Humphrey Noyes, a New England-born reformer who
believed he had personally attained sinless perfection, gathered
followers around him first in Vermont and then in upstate New
York. Noyes' Oneida colony was based on self-perfection,
communal economics, and "complex" (communal) marriage.
Many other, less famous colonies lived and died during the first
half of the nineteenth century, including agricultural cooperatives, "free love" experiments, spiritualist communities, and
one attempt to recreate a genteel English village in the hills
of Tennessee.

With the Civil War, the divisive and tumultuous era of
Reconstruction, and the growth of more conventional reform
movements, utopian experiments diminished during the 1860s
and 1870s. But the economic transformation of American
society that began to be felt in the late nineteenth century—
urbanization, growing dependence on machines, the hazards of
the factory system, and the increasingly unequal distribution of
wealth—brought new and more strident demands for reform.
Although European Marxism found its way to America via the
Socialist Labor Party, the "homegrown socialism" of men like
Edward Bellamy and Julius Wayland had a more widespread
effect on utopian thinking.

In 1887 Bellamy wrote *Looking Backward*, a novel depicting a
perfect urban society. Here unequal distribution of wealth was
replaced by economic equality; machines performed menial
labor while providing comfort and entertainment; a central
government functioned quietly and smoothly; culture and
refinement abounded. More than 200,000 copies of the book

were sold in its first three years of publication. Bellamy or Nationalist clubs were organized in 27 states, and dozens of Bellamy-inspired colonies sprang up. Julius Wayland was another proponent of native socialism. A rural reformer who founded several Populist newspapers, Wayland put his ideas into practice by establishing a working model of socialism at Ruskin Colony in Tennessee. Although the colony was short-lived, Wayland's impact on the utopian movement was not. He continued to preach socialism, Populism, and utopianism through the pages of the largest-circulation radical newspaper of the time, his *Appeal of Reason*.

Other reformers contributed their plans and ideas, from Henry George's single tax doctrines to the muckrakers' attacks on industrial capitalism. Utopian novels appeared annually. Labor unions grew large and active. The Populist movement, urging marketing and purchasing cooperatives and a complete overhaul of the economic system, captured the imagination of millions of southern and midwestern farmers. The Social Gospel movement (Christian Socialism), preaching social awareness and the responsibility of the Church, appealed to reform-minded clergy and laity. Anarchism attracted a variety of followers, including both immigrants and native-born Americans. Some believed in collective ownership of property and the overthrow of the U.S. government. Others believed in the supremacy of individual rights. Still others formed ties with radical labor. Many put their ideals to work, establishing autonomous colonies in the South, Rocky Mountain states, and Northwest.

Radical reformists and utopians continued to organize experimental colonies through the turn of the century, but events of the twentieth century eventually put a halt to the diverse utopian movement. The assassination of President McKinley by a self-proclaimed anarchist did harm to the anarchist movement, creating dissension within anarchist colonies and tension between colonies and their neighbors. The pacifist beliefs held by a variety of utopians came under fire during World War I when the U.S. government harrassed and suppressed antiwar advocates. The Great Depression that followed was not a time for visionary thought or action. After decades of material deprivation during the 1930s and through the war years, midcentury Americans did not seem to be interested in experimenting with rigorous new lifestyles.

Moreover, affordable land had virtually disappeared, and two of the basic tenets of utopianism—collective ownership of property and equal distribution of wealth—were saddled with the stigma of communism.

It was not until the 1960s that the utopian movement reemerged. The new colonists, like their ideological ancestors of the mid- and late nineteenth century, were generally young, well-educated, middle-class people reacting against the social, political, and cultural norms of the time. Some established rural colonies, farming the land and engaging in cottage industries like the Amana and Oneida colonists of a century before. Some founded urban communes where income was shared and domestic work was divided equally. Others gathered around charismatic leaders forming autonomous religious sects like the seventeenth- and eighteenth-century colonists.

By the most conservative estimates, nearly 600 utopian communities were organized in the United States from the first Puritan experiment to the present day. Not every colony had the resources to or felt the need for publishing its own newspaper or journal, but many did. Imbued with the spirit of reform, convinced they had the answers to society's problems, anxious to convert others to their way of thinking, utopians wanted a forum for their ideas. Undoubtedly they would have preferred using the conventional media of their day to reach millions of people quickly and efficiently with their message. But the conventional press reflected the very norms and customs utopians were rejecting. Furthermore, it was not the style of the conventional press to print lengthy, complex discussions of ideology and philosophy, the kind of discussions utopians felt they needed to publish to convert others to their vision. To spread the word, they had to start their own journals.

FUNCTIONS OF THE UTOPIAN PRESS

Utopian publications ranged from cheaply printed broadsides to sophisticated quarterly journals. Most were the products of individual colonies, although some operated independently as mouthpieces for particular utopian schools of thought. All were labors of love. Editors and writers almost always worked for no recompense other than the satisfaction of producing their own journal; advertising was virtually nonexistent and circulation was limited. Typically, the publications drained rather than augmented the financial resources of the colony. Editors spent long hours writing, editing, typesetting, printing, and mailing their publications for one reason only: They were convinced they had something important to say.

Although editorial content of the publications varied according to philosophy and colony, most publications performed similar functions. In general, internal communication was not a function of the colony publication. Members lived in close quarters, often working and eating together. Colony news—comings and goings of members, special visitors, financial information—was communicated during meetings or informally over dinner. Colonies that shared particular philosophies (Fourierist or Owenite experiments, for example), did use their home-based publications to communicate internal news to other like-minded but distant colonies. But in general utopian publications attempted to speak to outsiders.

Editors saw their major function as spreading the word about the colony—its ideals, its operation, and its promise—to those not associated with their particular brand of utopianism. Lengthy philosophical discussions abounded, as did news of the practical operation of the colony. Editors repeatedly discoursed on the problems of modern society and the inequities of the current economic, political, and social systems. They offered remedies that, they were quick to point out, could be seen in the daily operation of their colony. In the pages of their newspapers and periodicals, editors expounded on the major reform movements of the day, sometimes praising them, sometimes dismissing them as superficial or short-term solutions to deeper problems. All of this they did with the aim of propagandizing for their cause. They hoped to convince readers—most often reform-minded citizens or radicals involved in other movements—that their philosophy and their colony held the key to a better life.

Many colony newspapers also functioned as recruitment tools. Not only did editors want to convince the unconverted about the rightness of their ideas, they wanted to attract new members. Life in many utopian colonies meant rigorous physical labor, intense daily involvement with scores of others, and ostracism and ridicule by neighboring communities. Not surprisingly, the attrition rate was high, and colonists were always looking for new, energetic members to keep the experiment alive. Even successful, filled-to-capacity colonies encouraged visitors, hoping their experiences would lead them to start off-shoot colonies.

Publications were also used to defend the colony against outside attacks. Politicians, clergy, and the press rarely paid attention to the colonies, but when they did it was to denounce their philosophies and deride their practices. Communal living, female equality, and "free love" practices were favorite targets. Editors steadfastly defended the actions of colony members and attempted to explain the philosophy behind the practice. But the publications rarely reached those who had read the original accusations, the disapproving neighbors, and so had little effect on the attitudes of the surrounding communities.

Publications also functioned as literary and artistic outlets for colony members and showcases for the thoughts and ideas of European reformers and utopians.

PRE-CIVIL WAR UTOPIANS
AND THEIR PUBLICATIONS

Owenism and the *New Harmony Gazette*

Robert Owen was a wealthy British manufacturer and philanthropist who began his utopian experiments in the first decade of the nineteenth century when he purchased a Manchester mill and instigated a variety of worker reforms. At the New Lanark mills, he banned child labor, initiated sickness and old age insurance, and created educational and recreational facilties for workers. A few years later in his book, *A New View of Society*, he contended that a person's character was wholly determined by environment, and that consequently improvement in living and working environments would lead to improvement of individual character and morals. Concluding from his own experiences as a reformer that the selfish environment created by capitalism was detrimental to the intellectual and moral improvement of humanity, he developed the idea of "villages of cooperation." In these self-contained, self-sufficient villages, a healthy physical environment, economic cooperation rather than competition, and a communal spirit would reshape the characters of the participants.

Imagining that America, where the democratic experiment was in full swing, would be receptive to social experimentation, Owen arrived in the United States in 1825 to set up his first village of cooperation. Along with his son, Robert Dale Owen, and a Scottish reformer, Frances (Fanny) Wright, he established a colony at New Harmony, Indiana, site of a former German Rappite settlement. He believed the rest of America would be converted by the example of New Harmony and that the moral idealism of the colony would lay the groundwork for a future society.

Five months after he founded New Harmony, Owen and his son started publishing the *New Harmony Gazette*, a weekly that lasted for 156 issues. Like the Owens, the paper was sublimely optimistic about both the future of the colony and the future of society. The *Gazette* did not focus on the daily operation of the colony, but instead offered its readers philosophical discussions that reflected the Owens' belief about human perfectability within self-contained cooperative environments. The paper's mission was enlightenment, recruitment, and boosterism. From 1825 to 1828, the *New Harmony Gazette* was a showcase for Owenite philosophy and a public relations tool for the colony. Within its first year of publication, the weekly managed to attract a number of new members to New Harmony and helped provide the impetus for the founding of six additional Owenite colonies. But none of the experiments lasted more than two years.

After the failure of New Harmony (the Owens were only slightly discouraged, believing that old habits of individualism were difficult to break), the *Gazette* continued to publish as the *New Harmony and Nashoba Gazette* under the editorship of Robert Dale Owen and Frances Wright. In 1828 Wright moved the paper to New York City, changed its name to the *Free Inquirer*, and continued publishing lengthy discussions of cooperation, communality, and the importance of environment to moral and intellectual growth. The *Inquirer* died in 1835, but another Owenite publication, *The Disseminator of Useful Knowledge*, continued spreading the word until 1841. A minor revival of Owenism in the 1840s led the the short-lived *Herald of the New Moral World and Millennial Harbinger* (1841-1842). Fifteen years after the death of the New Harmony experiment,

Owen's utopian ideas were still alive in the pages of this weekly.

Owenism, aided more by its various newspapers than its string of unsuccessful colonies, had a discernible effect on American society through the actions of its adherents and converts. Owen himself helped convert Indiana to the idea of free public education by establishing traveling libraries throughout the state. Fanny Wright went on to become a famous lecturer for women's rights, free inquiry in religion, birth control, and free public education. Robert Dale Owen, who served for four years in the House of Representatives, became a vocal Abolitionist. Two Englishmen, converted to Owenism by the *Free Inquirer*, went on to publish *The Working Man's Advocate* and *the Daily Sentinel and Young America*. These papers, which called for educational and land reform, an end to wage slavery, Abolition, and women's rights, were the backbone of a moderately successful New York state reformist organization, the Working Men's Party.

Transcendentalism and *The Dial*

While the Owens were calling for a purposeful and rational reorganization of society into cooperative villages, another group of utopians was proclaiming that intuition, not reason, was the path to human perfection and societal harmony. Transcendentalism, which held that God, man, and nature were inseparable, was simultaneously an intellectual, spiritual, literary, aesthetic, ethical, and religious movement. Reacting to the cold formalism of Unitarianism (which was, in itself, a reaction to the "hellfire and brimstone" beliefs of the Great Awakening), Transcendentalists believed that nature was the seat of all learning and the center of moral laws. From nature, humankind received spiritual sustenance, inspiration, protection, and the means to live in harmony with the universe. One learned from nature not by study but by revelation. Like the Owenites, the Transcendentalists believed in human perfectability—but the key was individual growth through intuitive understanding, not structured communal life.

The first meeting of what would become the Transcendental Club, from which would emerge *The Dial*, took place in Boston in the fall of 1836. There four young and unhappy Unitarian ministers, including Ralph Waldo Emerson and George Ripley, met to discuss their dissatisfaction with the church. Throughout the late 1830s, the group continued to meet regularly, expanding its membership to include Boston educator Amos Bronson Alcott (father of the author Louisa May Alcott), Unitarian clergyman William Henry Channing, reformer and writer Margaret Fuller, educator and author Elizabeth Peabody, and social reformer Sarah Ripley. Although the group soon began discussing the possibility of a literary and journalistic vehicle to disseminate their ideas, their quarterly journal, The Dial, did not begin publication until July 1840.

The group apparently first considered other avenues for their transcendental discourses, but literary magazines did not deem them worthy and religious magazines closed their pages to the "new heretics." Early in 1840, Margaret Fuller, who was to be editor or co-edtitor of The Dial for most of its four years, wrote to a friend that the new journal would be a "perfectly free organ ... offered for the expression of individual thought and character." Reflecting the individualistic nature of the Transcendentalists' beliefs, she wrote: "I trust ... that this journal will aim, not at leading public opinion, but at stimulating each man to judge for himself, and to think more deeply and nobly." In May 1840, Fuller, Emerson, and George Ripley issued a prospectus for their new publication, stating that its purpose was to "furnish a medium for the freest expression of thought." Its contributors, they wrote, would "possess little in common but the love of individual freedom and the hope for social progress." In fact, they had much more in common: youth (editors, contributors, and writers were all in their late 20s to mid-30s), a philanthropic commitment to the journal (editors were unsalaried and contributors were unpaid), and a belief in the utopian philosophy of Transcendentalism.

The first issue of The Dial, appearing in the summer of 1840 under Fuller's editorship, established an editorial mix it was to maintain for the next four years: philosophical treatises, critical essays, literary criticism, and poetry. Although later historians were to call it "the literary gazette of a new spirit" and a novel, original, and courageous journal, contemporary reviewers either ignored The Dial or ridiculed it. Except for the Boston Times, which called The Dial "one of the most ridiculous productions of the age," and the *Boston Quarterly Review*, which called it "sickly, fungous literature," the press in *The Dial's* hometown disregarded the new publication, and the religious magazines of the day studiously ignored its existence. The *Philadelphia Gazette* called the journal's contributors "zanies" who were "considerably madder than the Mormonites." Only one newspaper was kind to the new publication. The New York *Tribune*, under its idiosyncratic reform-minded publisher Horace Greeley, gave free advertising space to *The Dial*.

Regardless of the lack of recognition and respect it commanded from its journalistic contemporaries, *The Dial* served to broaden the scope of the small Transcendentalist Club. It exported their philosophy beyond the confines of the Boston group, attracting contributors and readers from other parts of the country. It gave Transcendentalists an opportunity to clarify their thoughts and helped them to understand what their own cause meant to themselves and others. But *The Dial* never reached more than a few hundred subscribers.

One month before the first issue of *The Dial* was published, Fuller wrote to Emerson telling him that the journal had so far secured only 30 subscribers. The first issue probably reached fewer than 100 subscribers, and two years later *The Dial's* subscription list included only 220 names. But the extent of its influence on utopian thought is better measured by who subscribed and participated rather than by how many. *The Dial's* contributors and readers were active members of the intelligentsia who later had a major influence on the utopian and reform movements of their day. Margaret Fuller continued her work as a literary critic and became one of the most sophisticated and respected proponents of female equality. Ralph Waldo Emerson, who went on to achieve an international reputation as an essayist, poet, and lecturer, became an ardent Abolitionist. Horace Greeley continued to champion certain utopian experiments in the *Tribune* and, for a brief time, became a colony member himself. Amos Bronson Alcott, who called himself a "paradise planter," established a utopian colony called Fruitlands. George Ripley founded the great Transcendentalist experiment at Brook Farm, and William Henry Channing was instrumental in transforming Brook Farm into a Fourierist community.

Fourierism and *The Phalanx*

While the Transcendentalists were publishing *The Dial* and attempting a communal experiment at Brook Farm, Massachusetts, followers of the French social scientist and reformer Charles Fourier were busy creating their own version of utopia. Fourier, who devoted his life to studying society and devising methods of improving social and economic conditions, advocated the cooperative organization of society into "phalansteries" or "phalanxes." He envisioned a society divided into 1,600-person economically and socially self-sufficient groups in which each individual would be assigned work suitable to his or her personality. Fourier claimed that life in the phalanx would lead to the uniting of mind and body, thought and action, and man and nature. What was wrong with modern society, he claimed, was that these naturally harmonious forces were unnaturally separated.

Fourierism, also called Associationism, was one of the most popular utopian ideas of the time. During the 1840s and 1850s 40 different colonies were established in the northern United States. Horace Greeley, a Fourier enthusiast who served as treasurer of the North American Phalanx, helped popularize Associationism by running a regular column on the subject in his New York *Tribune* in 1842. But Greeley was the exception. The other newspapers of the day ignored or poked fun at Fourierism. To spread Associationism and to recruit new colonists, a small group of American Fourierists began publishing *The Phalanx* in 1843.

A solidly packed 16-page newspaper, *The Phalanx* proclaimed itself "devoted to the cause of Association or Social Reform and the Elevation of the Human Race." The front page was filled with slogans: "Political, social and religious unity"; "Social progress—a social reform upon conservative principles"; "Social and political liberty and quality"; "Association, Attractive Industry, Unity of Interests." "Our evils," ran another motto on the front page, "are social, not political, and a social reform can eradicate them." Under the editorship of Arthur Brisbane, author of several books on Fourierism and the man who wrote the *Tribune* column in 1842, *The Phalanx* published lengthy treatises on the system of Associationism as well as copious translations of Fourier's work. It offered critical essays on what the editor called "the present false system of society," and attempted to expose such societal evils as slavery, poverty, and the degradation of the working class.

Not tied to any particular phalanx, *The Phalanx* was the national journal of Fourierism in America. It included detailed coverage of Fourierist conventions, reports from individual colonies, correspondence from Fourierists in America and abroad, and earnest letters to the editor from various supporters. Greeley and Transcendentalist William Henry Channing were regular contributors.

The newspaper was distributed to all phalanxes and sold to Fourierist supporters throughout the United States. But its distribution to the unconverted was limited. Then early in 1844, a Louisiana Fourierist sent in money to subsidize six-month subscriptions to *The Phalanx* for the senior class of all 103 U.S. colleges and universities then in existence. The paper continued publishing somewhat irregularly—probably because of other commitments and duties of its editor and contributors—until May of 1845, when Brisbane announed that a new publication would take its place, *The Harbinger*.

Brook Farm and *The Harbinger*

Brook Farm in West Roxbury, Massachusetts was an outgrowth of the Boston Transcendentalist Club. Founded by George Ripley in 1841, a year after *The Dial* began publishing, it was a rather formless experiment in communal living. Some of the Boston Transcendentalists, their friends, and assorted itinerant intellectuals lived and worked together at Brook Farm for the purpose of communing with nature and, according to the Transcendentalist belief, gaining intuitive insight into man and God. The experiment, which lacked the organization and specific day-to-day purpose of most of the earlier colonies, was satirized by one of the wandering intellectuals who briefly made Brook Farm his home. Ten years after his stay at the colony, Nathaniel Hawthorne wrote the semifictional *The Blythdale Romance*, in which a naive poet rambled the grounds pontificating about nature while a farmer worked and belched. Lampooning the Transcendentalists' notion that nature could provide intellectual and spiritual fodder, Hawthorne wrote: "Clods of earth did not become thoughts, rather thoughts became cloddish."

Whether the other Brook Farm participants shared Hawthorne's amused skepticism is not known, but in 1844, under
the influence of William Henry Channing—Unitarian-turned-
Transcendentalist-turned-Associationist—the colony voted in a
new constitution making it a Fourierist phalanx. The last issue of
The Phalanx in spring 1845 announed that Brook Farm would
now publish the major Fourierist journal. *The Harbinger,* edited
by Ripley and published weekly from June 1844 to January
1849, became the most important Fourierist journal and one of
the best reform publications of its time. Simultaneously the
official organ of Brook Farm and the national Fourierist newspaper, *The Harbinger* boasted this motto: "The elevation of the
whole human race, in mind, morals and manners ... [by]
orderly and progressive reform." In its four years, it published
numerous articles by Ripley, Channing, Margaret Fuller, and
Charles Dana, one of Brook Farm's directors who was later to
write for Greeley's *Tribune* and, after abandoning his reform
interests in the 1860s, was to take over ownership of the New
York *Sun.*

The Harbinger proposed to study and discuss the great questions in social science, politics, literature, and the arts. In
politics, it proclaimed itself "democratic in its principles and
tendencies" and dedicated to the "happiness of the masses."
As the leading journal of Associationism, it was devoted to
Fourier's version of radical, organic social reform embodied in
the phalanx system. Editor Ripley explained it well in an
early essay:

> We have often been asked, What do friends of the Association
> propose to themselves, in the reform to which they are
> dedicated? Let me answer in a few words—by the systematic
> organization of labor, to make it more efficient, productive and
> attractive; in this way to provide for the abundant gratification of
> all intellectual, moral and physical wants of every member of the
> Association; and thus extirpate the dreadful inequities of
> external condition, which now make many aspects of society so
> hideous; and to put all in possession of the means of leading a
> wise, serene and beautiful life, in accordance with the eternal
> laws of God and the highest aspirations of their own nature.

In essay after essay Ripley wrote about human nature, the
influence of modern society, and Fourierist principles as they

could be adapted to America. Like the Owenites before him, Ripley believed that the evil he saw in the human race—selfishness, indifference to truth, hypocrisy, insane devotion to wealth, violence—was a product of modern society, not human nature. Ripley and others wrote optimistically and ebulliently about phalanx life, although they devoted little space to the specific goings on at Brook Farm. Like *The Phalanx, The Harbinger* aimed at a national audience covering important Fourierist conventions and lectures. How many people read the journal is unknown, but Fourierists made concerted efforts to circulate their publication. Among the duties listed for the officers of the national organization, the American Union of Associationists, was circulating *The Harbinger* and procuring subscriptions. According to accounts written by a Brook Farm member, visiting lecturers often toured the Northeast attempting to sell subscriptions.

When Brook Farm disbanded in 1847, Ripley took *The Harbinger* to New York, where he continued publishing it for another two years. Later he became the literary critic for Greeley's *Tribune*, the founder of *Harper's* magazine and co-editor, with Charles Dana, of the *New American Cyclopedia*. With the death of *The Harbinger*, William Henry Channing attempted to keep Fourierism alive by publishing *The Spirit of the Age*, a New York-based weekly that lasted until the spring of 1850.

The Oneida Community and Its Publications

The longest-lived and most financially successful utopian experiment of the time was the colony founded by Vermont-born reformer and preacher John Humphrey Noyes. After a conversion experience in his early 20s, Noyes announced that he had achieved sinless perfection and that he would show others how to follow in his footsteps. In 1834 he gathered a small group of believers in Putney, Vermont and began an experiment based on human perfectability through communal property, community living, and group marriage. Noyes saw monogamous marriage, like private property, as an expression of selfishness and possessiveness. In the Putney colony, established in 1836, both people and goods were to be shared. Every man and woman in the colony was "married" to each other—he called it complex marriage—and community love was encouraged. To control unwanted births, Noyes preached "coitus reservatus" and later expanded his views in a lengthy treatise on male continence.

In 1838 Noyes, his legal wife, and several of his brothers and sisters began publishing *The Witness* to disseminate Noyes' views and attact followers. The weekly paper—written, edited, typeset, and mailed by the Noyes family for almost ten years—included discussions of self-perfection, communalism, and group marriage as well as explanations of the workings of the Putney experiment. By the mid-1840s, the Putney colony numbered 50 people and was the talk of the town. In 1846 Noyes was arrested because of the colony's free love practices and was hounded by his neighbors until he moved the colony to upstate New York in 1848, renaming it Oneida Community.

In New York the community flourished. Wealthy new members divested themselves of their personal property, and within the next ten years more than $100,000 was invested in Oneida. The community had brick buildings, a photographic studio, a chemical laboratory, a Turkish bath, and library stocked with 6,000 books. By 1870 Oneida included more than 300 members who lived in comfortable buildings and operated several prosperous industries, including the production of the famous Oneida silverware. But early on the transplanted colonists were worried about public relations. Their reputation for sexual permissiveness had gotten them into trouble in Vermont, and they wanted their neighbors and others to understand what they were doing and why. To do this they began publishing a colony newspaper.

First called the *Free Church Circular* and published semi-weekly, it was soon changed to a weekly called the *Oneida Circular*. From 1851 to 1876 it published Noyes' views and community news. Aimed at both outsiders and fellow utopians, the newspaper reached a peak circulation of 2,000, in part because it was given away free to those who could not afford the $2 annual subscription fee. But the community was wealthy enough to support this journalistic effort for 25 years. Oneida continued for several years after the death of the *Circular*, abandoning the idea of complex marriage in 1879 and incorporating itself in 1881.

POST-CIVIL WAR UTOPIANS
AND THEIR PUBLICATIONS

Utopian experiments in the late nineteenth and early twentieth centuries, like those in the pre-Civil War period, were based on the broad notion that a perfect environment would create perfect individuals. But no single, carefully worked out philosophy like Owenism, Fourierism, or the ideas of Noyes captured the imagination of American radicals and reformers. The major reform ideas of the time—the Social Gospel, socialism, and anarchism—were so loosely defined as to allow the formation of dozens of communal experiments that had little in common with each other.

Some experiments, like the Rugby Colony in Morgan County, Tennessee, were one-of-a-kind ventures. Here members created a working replica of an old English village with the idea that the hard American countryside and the genteel English village life would forge a self-reliant but civilized society. *The Rugbian*, the colony's monthly journal, chronicled the experiment from 1880 to 1889. Near Bakersfield, California, the *Joyful News Co-operator* detailed life at the Association of Brotherly Co-operators, a commune organized around vegetarianism, temperance, and women's rights. Other colony newspapers, from *The Star of Hope* in Kansas to the *Cooperative Colonist* in Nevada, helped spread utopian visions while recruiting new members and bolstering the morale of colonists.

Colonies Inspired by Utopian Writers

One of the literary responses to the so-called Gilded Age, a time of great labor unrest and socioeconomic inequities, was the utopian novel. This genre gave late nineteenth-century writers an opportunity to criticize modern society while creating visions of a perfect world. It is impossible to determine how many, if any, readers of Ignatius Donnelly's *Caesar's Column* were inspired by his vision of a pastoral paradise made possible through public philanthropy and universal suffrage. But at least two utopian novels were directly responsible for the founding of colonies that attempted to mirror their fictional worlds.

William Dean Howells was a poet, magazine editor (*Harper's, Atlantic Monthly, Cosmopolitan*), and author of more than 20 books of fiction. Among these was *A Traveler from Altruria*, a utopian novel about a distant civilization. In Altruria, a classless society cut off from the contaminating influences of urban life, people farmed the land, lived cooperatively, and participated fully in their own governance. The novel sparked a series of Altruria clubs throughout California and at least two colonies, Altruria in Sonoma County and the Colorado Cooperative Colony. Like Howells' fictional society, these colonies were organized around communal agricultural labor, community property, and democratic suffrage. The California colony published *The Altrurian*, a weekly newspaper, during the one-year life of the experiment. The more successful Colorado colony also published a journal called *The Altrurian* from 1894 to 1910.

Probably the most important utopian novel of the time was Edward Bellamy's *Looking Backward*, the book that sold more than 200,000 copies in its first three years. Unlike Altruria, Bellamy's utopia was urban; it was, in fact, his vision of Boston in the year 2000. He envisioned a self-sufficient, classless, cooperative society in which modern machines were used to make life carefree. Within a year after the book's publication, several dozen Bellamy or Nationalist Clubs were formed, and a movement magazine was started. *The Nationalist*, which published from 1889 to 1891, acted as a national journal for the Bellamy-inspired movement, keeping clubs informed of one another's activities and discussing the ideas of cooperative economics. Bellamy himself was not pleased with the magazine and started his own, *The New Nation*, late in 1889. More reformer than utopian, he used his magazine to promote Populism and public ownership of railroads and utilities.

Henry George was neither a utopian nor a novelist, but his *Progress and Poverty* led to the founding of a number of clubs, two journals, at least one colony, and a political party. While working in San Francisco as a typesetter and later an editor, George studied the California land boom following the development of the railraod and formed his single tax theory. He believed that all inequities of wealth, power, and privilege stemmed from the right of the few to monopolize the rising value that society as a whole bestowed on land. Property-holders need only sit back and watch the value of their land increase as society grew up around them. The land, said George, should be taxed, and the tax revenues divided among the people. This single tax would destroy monopoly power and lead to social progress and harmony. Followers of the single tax doctrine organized into clubs throughout the nation, and in 1890 a midwestern professor of mathematics began publishing *Opinion and Outlook*, a single tax journal, in Des Moines, Iowa. Five years later he moved to Alabama to become the leader of Fairhope, a colony that tried to put George's theory to work. George's ideas also inspired *Single Taxer*, the early twentieth-century organ of the Single Tax Party.

The Social Gospel

Utopian novels were a literary response to the social and economic inequities of post-Civil War America; the Social Gospel was a theological response. Looking at the hazards of the factory system, the growing gulf between rich and poor, and the escalating conflict between capital and labor, some Protestant leaders believed Christianity and the Church needed redefinition. Their movement was called the Social Gospel or Christian Socialism. Emerging from the Unitarian, Episcopalian, and Congregationalist churches, the Social Gospel called for the application of the teachings of Jesus Christ to society, economic life, social institutions, and the individual. Social Gospel leaders blamed the conflict between business and labor for societal problems and saw competition as a form of warfare that brutalized society and devastated the moral order. They believed that love, brotherhood, and cooperation—the message of Christ—should be applied to the entire social order.

To achieve this, the clergy proposed that the Church formulate a program of action and progressive theology that would meet the needs and concerns of the masses. Trusting the power of the Church, Social Gospel leaders did not call for a restructuring of social organization. But a variety of middle-class reformers used the tenets of the Social Gospel to do just that, establishing a number of experimental communities and starting publications to spread the word.

The Willard Co-operative Colony, named after temperance leader Frances Willard, was one such colony. Its efforts were publicized in a late nineteenth-century reform periodical called *The Kingdom*. A few years later, the editor of that journal joined the Christian Commonwealth Colony in Georgia and began publishing *The Social Gospel*, a colony newspaper that reached 2,000 readers. Both colonies and both publications were based on the idea that love, brotherhood, and the Kingdom of Heaven could be realized on earth by living according to the teachings of Christ. At the Georgia colony, which included almost 100 members, they called it "practical Christianity."

In Michigan, Christian Socialists founded Hiawatha Village, a farming colony based on community property, communal work, and the teachings of Christ. From 1893 to 1896 colony members published *The Industrialist Christian* in an attempt to disseminate their ideas. In New Jersey, the Straight Edge Industrial Settlement ran a bakery, a print shop, a day care center, and for 22 years published *The Straight Edge*. The colony described itself as "a school of methods for the application of the teachings of Jesus to Business and Society," and its publication discoursed on these ideas.

Utopias of the Northwest

From the 1820s to the 1850s, a heyday for utopian communities, most colonies could be found in the Northeast and Midwest. But by the end of the nineteenth century, a variety of colonies began to crop up in the northwest corner of the nation. Unlike the more settled and developed eastern regions, in the Northwest at the turn of the century, open, affordable land was still available. Cities, which many utopians believed to be environments hostile to human progress and perfection, were small, few, and far between. In general, the Northwest had been kind to reform movements; Knights of Labor, the Grange, Populism, and various labor organizations (including, in the early twentieth century, the radical Industrial Workers of the World) were active and visible. Geographically—and perhaps psychologically as well—the Northwest was the farthest utopians could go to get away from the social, economic, and political evils they associated with the East Coast metropolises.

During the late nineteenth and early twentieth centuries, the Puget Sound area in Washington was home to a half-dozen new communal experiments. Regional historian Charles Pierce LeWarne devoted an entire book, *Utopias on Puget Sound*, to these experiments. All were self-contained colonies organized around the concept of cooperative labor. All involved at least some degree of communal living, and most believed in community property. Perhaps most important, all were active journalistically.

The Brotherhood of Cooperative Commonwealth (BCC) was a group of utopian socialists who saw the creation of individual utopian communities as the first step toward converting the whole country to socialism. The group helped found two Puget Sound colonies based on common production, distribution, and consumption of goods: Equality and Burley. In 1897, the 15 members of the new Equality colony were busy clearing land, building, and planting crops, but they were still conscious of their wider socialist mission. Unable to start their own publication immediately, they used the pages of *The Coming Nation*, probably the largest-circulation radical newspaper of the time, to publicize the new colony and discuss its goals. Less than six months later, the colony began publishing its own newspaper, *Industrial Freedom*. Edited by a reform-minded Minnesota newspaperman who brought his type, press, and printing equipment with him when he joined Equality, the newspaper acted as a bulletin for BCC news as well as a forum for socialist ideas in general. The paper, which was published from 1898 to 1902, contained official news and unofficial gossip about Equality and the BCC, articles on a variety of reform measures, and correspondence with socialists and reformers around the country. At times the BCC used *Industrial Freedom* to offer assistance to socialists anywhere who wished to start their own colonies.

The BCC's second Puget Sound colony, Burley, began in 1898. Immediately after the handful of colonists cleared the land, they began publishing a newspaper. *The Co-operator*, issued in various formats and under several editors, continued for eight years, longer than any other single journal to come from the Puget Sound colonies. At first the editor set up his press in the living room of an abandoned house with the type cases stacked in the bedroom. Later the paper moved to a two-story printing office built by Burley colonists. First a tabloid weekly, later a 32-page (and then 16-page) monthly, *The Co-operator* was similar in content to *Industrial Freedom*. It carried discussions of socialism and other reform movements, news of Burley and the BCC, and information about other communitarian experiments. *The Co-operator* was not the only product of Burley's printing office; it also produced *Soundview*, a "Magazine Devoted to the Obstetrics of Thought and the Philosophy of Existence." The monthly was filled with radical and esoteric subjects, anecdotes, comments, and book reviews.

Two disaffected colonists, one from Burley and one from Equality, founded another experiment called Freeland on Whidby Island in the Puget Sound. The founders, believing that "communism on a small scale is a failure," established a profit-sharing, interest-paying association in which members bought shares of land and owned stock in the colony store and colony steamboat. Freeland's 1900 charter specified that one of the colony's activities should be "to construct, own, manage and operate . . . the business of printing and the publication of newspapers, periodicals, books and means of advertising." The *Whidby Islander*, founded eight months after Freeland was incorporated, became the unofficial colony newspaper. Offering gossip about the colony written by "The Association Crank" and "The Devil Himself," it agitated for equal distribution of wealth and property and tried to promote the growth of the colony by carrying advertising for Whidby Island real estate.

The most famous, longest-lived, and most journalistically prolific Puget Sound experiment was the anarchist colony of Home. Called a "collection of outlaws," an "unclean den of infamy" and a "nest of vipers" by its Tacoma neighbors, Home was built on commonly held land but included privately owned houses. More a loose collection of individuals than a communal association, Home prided itself on its commitment to individual liberty and freedom from all laws. One of Home's earliest settlers, Oliver A. Verity, realized that the success of the venture would depend on publicizing the colony and its philosphy. Shortly after his arrival in 1896, he appealed to fellow radicals in the pages of *The Coming Nation*. A year later, he issued the first newspaper from Home, *New Era*, which he used to describe the community and advertise for colonists. Printed on a used hand-operated press that printed only a half-page at a time, *New Era* was distributed throughout radical circles.

A copy of the paper found its way to a San Francisco saloon where wandering printer Charles L. Govan read it and decided to come to Home. By the time he arrived, *New Era* had died, but he and Verity almost immediately began a second paper, *Discontent: The Mother of Progress*. A four-page tabloid, the weekly was not the official organ of Home, although it attempted to arouse interest in the colony and attract members. It was, instead, an open forum for anarchist ideas, pledging itself to "battle for the freedom of the human race from tyranny and superstition." For four years it discussed politics, economics, religion, world affairs, and sex, keeping its eye on the national and international anarchist movements. In 1903 it changed its name to *The Demonstrator* and continued publishing for another five years. From 1910 to 1912 Home was the site of yet another anarchist publication, the twice-monthly *Agitator*. Edited by a well-known anarchist who had been wounded in the Haymarket Riots, the paper advocated industrial unionism and individual freedom.

One way the locally unpopular anarchist community was harassed was by government interference in the publication and distribution of its journals. Ten days after a self-proclaimed anarchist assassinated President McKinley, federal officials arrived at Home to arrest the editors of *Discontent* for mailing obscene literature under provisions of the 1873 Comstock Act. The obscene literature was actually an excerpt from a well-known tract denouncing monogamous marriage as hypocritical. The Tacoma judge who heard the case the following year deemed the material "radical" but not obscene. The jury disagreed, and the editors were fined $100. Later that year, after subscribers complained they were not receiving their copies of *Discontent*, an investigation showed that the Tacoma Post Office was not mailing the publication. In 1911 the editor of *The Agitator* was arrested for printing an editorial supporting Home colonists' right to swim in the nude. In a locally famous case dubbed "the nudes and the prudes," the editor was found guilty of "advocating disrespect for the law" by a Tacoma jury. He served two months in jail.

The Puget Sound colonies' publications, like many other utopian journals, attempted to be national forums for radical and reformist ideas. Although none of these journals succeeded in their primary purpose—converting the rest of society to their utopian schemes—some utopian ideas did eventually find their way into mainstream society. Progressive reformers and politicians in the early twentieth century succeeded in passing legislation that blunted the power of monopolies and improved the conditions of working people. Later in the century, Franklin D. Roosevelt's New Deal legislation established the concept of government involvement in the lives of its less fortunate citizens. The basic utopian ideas of shared property and communal labor did not, however, find wide acceptance in a society that strongly believed in individual initiative and practiced conspicuous consumption. But the utopian dream persisted.

MODERN-DAY UTOPIAS

In the late 1960s, middle-class radicals and reformers once again reacted to what they saw as the evils of their day by establishing self-contained communal societies. Interestingly, both their critique of mainstream culture and their visions of utopia were indistinguishable from those of the nineteenth-century radicals. Like their ideological ancestors, modern-day utopians saw competition, possessiveness, and the increasing depersonalization of a highly mechanized society as evils. Their solution was the founding of self-sufficient colonies based on communal property, shared labor, social equality, self-development, and individual freedom. As in the pre-Civil War days, some colonies organized themselves around a single charismatic leader, while others were loose associations of like-minded individuals. In the 1830s and 1840s American radicals were attracted to the European philosophies of Owen and Fourier. In the 1960s and 1970s, eastern ideas—Buddhism, Zen, Sikhism, Sufism, Hare Krishna—gained popularity and became the bases for scores of communal experiments. New communes sprouted throughout the country, from New Hampshire to New Mexico, from Tennessee to Oregon. Some were agricultural, some operated cottage industries, some were artistic, some were spiritual. Most, like their nineteenth-century predecessors, were short-lived.

Few, if any, started their own publications. The cost of paper, presses, and postage was more than most communes could support. But several national journals did appear to spread the word. *The Whole Earth Catalog*, in between information on tools and products for self-sufficient living, offered news of new communities and new ideas. *Seriatim*, billing itself as "The Journal of Ecotopia" (futurist Ernest Callenbach's vision of a self-sufficient region in the Northwest), presented articles on appropriate technology, organic farming, and herbal medicine. *Communities* kept track of new colonies and their philosophies. *Alternative Futures* promoted interdisciplinary research into communal history and served as an intellectual focus for utopian scholarship.

More than 350 years after the Puritans attempted to create their vision of a perfect world, Americans were still searching for utopia.

REFERENCES

The following material aided in the preparation of this chapter and is suggested for further reading:

Bestor, Arthur. *Backwoods Utopias*. Philadelphia: University of Pennsylvania Press, 1950.

Carden, Maren Lockwood. *Oneida: Utopian Community to Modern Corporation*. Baltimore: Johns Hopkins University Press, 1969.

Codman, John Thomas. *Brook Farm, Historic and Personal Memoirs*. Boston: Arena, 1894.

Cooke, George Willis. *An Historical and Biographical Introduction to Accompany The Dial*. Cleveland: The Rowfant Club, 1902.

Fogarty, Robert S. *Dictionary of American Communal and Utopian History*. Westport, CT: Greenwood Press, 1980.

Holloway, Mark. *Heavens on Earth*. New York: Library Publishers, 1951.

Lawson, Donna. *Brothers and Sisters All Over This Land*. New York: Praeger, 1972.

LeWarne, Charles Pierce. *Utopias on Puget Sound, 1885-1915*. Seattle: University of Washington Press, 1975.

Myerson, Joel. *The New England Transcendentalists and The Dial.* Canbury, NJ: Associated University Press, 1980.

Nordhoff, Charles. *The Communistic Societies of the United States.* New York: Hillary House Publishers, 1961.

The Phalanx. New York: Burt Franklin, 1967.

Sams, Henry W., ed. *Autobiography of Brook Farm.* Englewood Cliffs, NJ: Prentice-Hall, 1958.

Veysey, Laurence. *The Communal Experience: Anarchist and Mystical Counter-cultures in America.* New York: Harper & Row, 1973.

4

A SIEGE OF THE CITADELS

They tell us sometimes that if we had only kept quiet, all these desirable things would have come about of themselves.

—Elizabeth Cady Stanton

Eight generations of American feminists have refused to keep quiet about inequality and discrimination. In their 150-year fight for political, social, and economic parity, they have used the few strategies available to them to further their cause. Denied basic political rights before the passage of the Nineteenth Amendment in 1920, women could not use the legislative process to fight for their rights. Excluded first from many of the professions, and even now from top decision-making positions, they could not work from within the system they wanted to change. Financially dependent on men, they could not wield economic power in their own service. Ignored, ridiculed, or stereotyped by the conventional media, they could not use this traditional forum for the presentation of their ideas.

Instead, they formed separate organizations, initiated lecture tours, called for demonstrations, and established their own journalistic voices. Only through these alternative means could feminists be assured an outlet for their ideas. From the first women's crusade of the 1840s to the current movement of the 1980s, feminist newspapers and periodicals have been the backbone of the ongoing women's movement. Serving as organizational tools, morale boosters, consciousness-raisers, philosophical and political forums, and propaganda organs, hundreds of these journals have helped wage the battle for equality.

THE FIRST FEMINIST MOVEMENT

In 1776, while the founding fathers were meeting to formulate a code of laws, Abigial Adams wrote to her husband John: "I desire you would remember the Ladies. . . . If particular care and attention is not paid to the Ladies, we are determined to foment a Rebellion." But the framers of the Constitution ignored her plea, and American women had to wage a separate battle for their independence. That they did not begin immediately may seem mysterious to late twentieth-century Americans, but it is understandable in the context of the time. Constrained by their society's definition of womanhood—women were believed to be morally superior to men but intellectually, emotionally, and physically inferior—early nineteenth-century women were isolated in their domestic sphere. With virtually no opportunity to experience public life, they had litte confidence in their ability to speak for themselves. The law told them married women were the property of their husbands. Society told them umarried women were unnatural creatures. Given these constraints, it is remarkable that the women's movement began at all.

In 1792, the year the first "woman's magazine" was published—a genteel, literary effort called *The Lady's Magazine*—Mary Wollstonecraft wrote the first feminine declaration of independence. Calling for "justice for one half of the human race" and "participation in the natural rights of mankind," her "Vindication of the Rights of Women" served as both an inspiration for nineteenth-century feminists and a call to arms. But it took American women almost 60 years to answer the call.

The first feminist movement emerged from the crusade against slavery, with Abolitionist papers providing the earliest forum for the discussion of feminist ideas. Important journals like *The Liberator* and *The North Star* called for the enfranchisement of women. The Abolition movement brought its female participants—many of whom were also feminists—out of domestic isolation and into public life, allowing them to gain expertise as organizers, writers, and speakers. Still, women Abolitionists were not considered equal to their male counterparts, and at the 1840 World Anti-Slavery convention in London they were denied participation. Elizabeth Cady Stanton and

Lucretia Mott, two of the women who traveled to London but who were excluded from the convention, spent their days discussing Wollstonecraft's essay and devising a plan for the first women's rights convention. Eight years later, their plans were realized.

On July 20, 1848, when 68 women and 2 men met in Seneca Falls, New York, the American women's movement was born. The document written at Seneca Falls mimicked the language of the Declaration of Independence, proclaiming that "all men and *women* are created equal" and went on to list a host of grievances against men, the first of which read: "He has never permitted her to exercise her inalienable right to the elective franchise.

After Seneca Falls, feminist newspapers emerged to further the cause. Amelia Bloomer's *Lily* began as a temperance publication in 1849, but less than a year later, under the influence of Elizabeth Cady Stanton, it started emphasizing suffrage. By 1852, the eight-page monthly, which at its height reached 6,000 subscribers, was completely given over to the fight for women's enfranchisement. Paulina Wright Davis, organizer of the first national suffrage convention in 1850, attempted to attract sophisticated, intellectual readers with *Una*. From 1853 to 1856 the publication presented women's issues in learned, philosophical articles written in a dignified and detached tone. *The Sibyl* in New York and *The Pioneer and Woman's Advocate* in Rhode Island were two other pre-Civil War feminist journals.

THE SECOND WAVE OF FEMINISM

Women's rights leaders had put away their cause for the duration of the war, believing that when peace came, they, along with Blacks, would be enfranchised. Thus the 1868 ratification of the Fourteenth Amendment came as a shock. For the first time, the world "male" appeared in the U.S. constitution. Together, the Fourteenth and Fifteenth Amendments meant that voting rights, which had been considered a state matter, were part of federal law and women were expressly excluded. Feminists understood they would have a long fight ahead of them. Organizing and lecturing activities began immediately, and women's rights newspapers sprang up across the nation.

The first and most famous of these post-Civil War papers was the short-lived *The Revolution*. Published by Susan B. Anthony, edited by Elizabeth Cady Stanton, and financed by wealthy eccentric Francis Train, the 16-page weekly lived up to its name. In the first issue on January 8, 1868, Stanton wrote:

> The enfranchisement of women is one of the leading ideas that calls this journal into existence. Seeing its realization, the many necessary changes in our modes of life, we think The Revolution a fitting name for a paper that will advocate so radical a reform as this involves in our political, religious and social worlds.

Calling for political enfranchisement as the first, basic right, *The Revolution* went on to argue for liberalized divorce laws, equal pay, and equal employment opportunities for women, unionization, and the elevation of the place of women in organized religion.

The Revolution may have been revolutionary, but *Woodhull and Claflin's Weekly* was considered downright scandalous. The joint venture of Victoria Woodhull and her sister Tennessee Claflin, the paper championed not only women's voting rights but Woodhull's candidacy for the president of the United States. It candidly discussed free love, prostitution, abortion, and venereal disease, alienating not only men but many feminists as well. More than 30 years later, Charlotte Perkins Gilman, one of the most respected feminist theorists of her time, was to write about these subjects in her newspaper, *The Forerunner*.

Woman's Journal took the opposite tack. Edited and published by Lucy Stone and her husband Henry Blackwell, the Boston-based paper appealed to moderates who supported the fight for women's enfranchisement but did not see the necessity for any other social or political reforms. Financially supported by various suffrage organizations, the *Journal* continued its one-issue stance from 1870 to 1917.

The leaders of the national suffrage movement—Stanton, Anthony, Stone, and others—lived and worked in the Northeast. But women's rights activities and feminist journalism knew no geographical boundaries. In San Francisco, Emily Pitts Stevens began publishing *The Pioneer* in 1869, proclaiming that "we shall insist upon women's independence—her elevation, socially and politically, to the platform now solely occupied by man." In

Portland, Oregon Abigail Scott Duniway began "a siege of the citadels of one-sexed government" with the publication of *New Northwest* in 1871. The following year *Women's Exponent* was issued from Utah. Midwest suffragist Clara Bewick Colby published *Woman's Tribune* from Beatrice, Nebraska, and other prosuffrage newspapers sprang up in Chicago, Denver, Toledo, Little Rock, and St. Petersburg.

The last two decades of the nineteenth century saw a spate of periodicals appealing to women's club members (there were more than 3,000 such clubs by the turn of the century) and professional women. Concerned both with women's rights activities and furthering women's intellectual and professional accomplishments, publications like *Journal of the American Association of University Women, The Business Woman's Journal,* and the *National Federation of Business and Professional Women's Club Bulletin* created new forums for the discussion of women's rights by spreading the word beyond avowed feminists to a broad range of middle-class women.

Margaret Sanger took another approach to feminism. To her, reproductive freedom superseded political rights. In 1914 she began publishing *The Woman Rebel* dedicated to the proposition that women should raise more hell and fewer babies. Primarily devoted to discussions of sex education and the medical and financial hazards of having large families, Sanger's journal also echoed the radical labor line of the International Workers of the World. In *The Woman Rebel,* Sanger referred to the "slavery of motherhood" and published an article by Emma Goldman calling marriage "a degenerate institution." But it was an article on contraception in the journal's second issue that got her into trouble. Although the article contained no specific advice on contraception, no discussion of anatomy, and no references to the sex act, it was declared "indecent, lewd, lascivious and obscene" under the Comstock Law. Sanger was indicted for sending birth control information (the newspaper and several pamphlets) through the mail. The prosecution, fearful that a public trial would make Sanger a martyr and lead to a public debate on contraception, dropped the case.

Sanger's efforts aside, most early twentieth-century feminists concentrated on the battle they and their mothers had been fighting since 1848: the constitutional right to vote. There had been scattered state victories throughout the West—Wyoming, Colorado, Utah, Idaho, Oregon, Washington, California—but feminists knew there would be no real victory until an amendment to the federal constitution guaranteed all women the right to vote. Dropping all other social and political reforms, national suffrage organizations escalated the fight. *The Suffragist*, the official weekly of Alice Paul's Congressional Union, was founded in 1913 for the sole purpose of working for a federal amendment. The National Women's Party, another militant organization headed by Paul, proposed an Equal Rights Amendment (the same amendment that remained unratified in the 1980s) and published *Equal Rights* in the early years of World War I. *The Woman Citizen*, published in the last years of the fight, covered congressional debates on the amendment.

When the Nineteenth Amendment finally became law in 1920, it was the culmination of an almost 80-year crusade for political equality that had been led by three generations of women and scores of feminist publications. The amendment changed women's political status, but it did nothing to alter their social or cultural position. Its passage signaled the end of one battle and the beginning of countless others.

SOCIAL FEMINISM OF THE 1920s

Feminism did not die after women won the right to vote. True, the national suffrage organizations disbanded, many of the suffrage journals ceased publication, and women no longer had one central rallying issue, but women of the 1920s strove to use their newly won citizenship to advance a number of reforms. Social feminists contributed their organizational and journalistic skills to the temperance and conservation movements and the crusades for child labor reform and pure food and drugs. Called "social housekeepers" because of their reform efforts were seen as extensions of their "primary role as mothers" beyond the family to society, female progressives continued to be constrained by society's definition of womanhood.

Margaret Sanger, expanding the crusade she began before World War I, wanted to change women's biologically limited horizons by providing them with birth control information. Her *Birth Control Review*, featuring articles by Karl Menninger, Pearl S. Buck, and Julian Huxley, discussed the personal and global implications of large families and provided its readers with the scant information then available on contraception. In step with the free-wheeling "flappers" of the 20s, Sanger also wrote and lectured on the joys of an active sex life.

The National League of Women Voters, calling for informed use of the franchise and participation in party politics, began publishing *Woman Citizen*. By the mid-1920s it was an independent journal that supported women candidates and editorialized for a host of progressive reforms including child labor laws and maternity leaves for working mothers. *Medical Woman's Journal* spoke to and for female doctors, supporting their professional efforts and joining in the progressive crusades for improved child care and personal hygiene. For female lawyers there was *Women Lawyers' Journal*, which also offered professional support to its readers. Organizations like the National Association of Bank Women and the National Women's Trade Union showed that feminists of the 1920s were far more than "social housekeepers."

FEMINISM IN THE 1930s AND 1940s

Although 25% of American women held paying jobs by the end of the 1920s, society's traditional definition of womanhood was not seriously challenged. Most women who worked outside the home were young, unmarried, and segregated in female-only jobs. New office technology led to the feminization of the workplace with women replacing men as secretaries, typists, and file clerks. During the Depression even these modest gains in women's economic independence were threatened. The ailing economy and massive unemployment hurt all workers, but women were a special target. Labor unions, federal and state governments, and the conventional media all joined in a campaign urging women to refrain from taking jobs. Women worked for "pin money"; men worked to support families—that was the erroneous but ubiquitous rationale.

But labor, government, and the conventional press did an about-face after the United States entered World War II. Now women workers were needed desperately. What is more, they were needed in jobs that women had been told for decades they were incapable of performing. The government, through the War Manpower Commission and the Women's Bureau of the Department of Labor, unwittingly became the strongest proponent of feminism since Susan B. Anthony and Elizabeth Cady Stanton issued *The Revolution.* To convince women they could handle jobs as welders, riveters, drill press operators, and foundry workers, government agencies issued pamphlets proclaiming: "If you can drive a car, you can run a machine." To convince employers to hire women, the War Manpower Commission published bulletins declaring that "women can do the job as well as men." A 1942 Office of War Information pamphlet told prospective employers that "women have proven their worth" by "performing excellently in high pressure production jobs." Government agencies carried out massive newspaper, magazine, and radio campaigns carrying the revolutionary message that women were just as capable as men of doing any job they were trained for.

Government publications and government-sponsored media campaigns went even further in promoting the cause of feminism. They called for equal pay, pregnancy leaves that did not jeopardize seniority, and day care facilities for working mothers. Other pamphlets asked merchants, dentists, and doctors to change their hours to make their services more convenient for working women. Feminists hardly needed journals of their own with the government and the conventional press furthering their cause.

Six million women took paying jobs during World War II, three-quarters of a million in the shipyards, two and a half million in aircraft plants, and millions more in the steel, automotive, and electrical industries. At the beginning of the war, 95% of working women said they intended to quit when the men came home. By the end of the war, 80% said they wanted to keep working. But two days after V-J day, 800,000 aircraft workers, mostly women, were fired. By the end of 1946, two million women were fired from jobs in heavy industry. Some companies reinstated their prewar policies against hiring women. The government halted its flirtation with feminism. Flying in the face of five years of feminist progaganda, the New York *Times* published an article by the dean of Barnard College stating that women "have a lower fatigue point and a less stable nervous system than men." The conventional press had changed its tune. Now a woman's place was at home and her true vocation was motherhood.

THE FEMININE MYSTIQUE

"Your task," presidential candidate Adlai Stevenson told the 1955 graduating class of Smith, "is to influence man and boy through the humble role of housewife." "Women must boldly announce that no job is more exciting, more necessary or more rewarding than that of housewife and mother," stated a 1950 *Atlantic* article. Declared *Saturday Review* in 1958: "Being a good wife, a good mother... is the most important of all occupations in the world." This was the message sent to the women of the 1950s. With no organized movement to challenge that message and no avowedly feminist periodicals to offer alternatives, women became victims of what Betty Friedan called "the feminine mystique."

With the huge circulation women's service magazines—*Ladies' Home Journal, McCall's, Woman's Day,* and *Good Housekeeping*—leading the way, women were told that "true feminine fulfillment" could only be achieved through husband, children, and home. A woman without a family was "abnormal." A dissatisfied housewife was "maladjusted." When Friedan analyzed issues of the three-million-plus circulation women's service magazines of the 1950s, she found that not one fictional heroine had a career. Only one in 100 had a job. She noted such stories as "An Encyclopedic Approach to Finding a Second Husband" as well as pages of models in maternity clothes. All the news of the "domestic sphere" was covered in full. There was no news of the outside world.

"Our readers," the editor of a large-circulation women's magazine told Friedan, "are not interested in the broad public issues of the day. They are not interested in national or international affairs. They are only interested in family and home." But by the close of the decade, the proportion of American women working outside the home increased to one out of three. The feminine mystique belied their experiences and aspirations. "I sensed it first as a question mark in my own life," wrote Friedan in 1963. By the end of the 1960s, millions of women would join her in questioning the limited role of their sex.

THE THIRD WAVE OF FEMINISM

Betty Friedan's *Feminine Mystique* and Simone de Beauvoir's *The Second Sex* may have set the stage for the rebirth of the feminist movement, but third-wave feminists were women of the 1960s, not the 1950s. Like their ideological ancestors of the 1840s, the new feminists also emerged from the major reform movements of their day: civil rights, antiwar, and student rights.

In 1964 Ruby Doris Robinson, one of the Student Non-Violent Coordinating Committee's (SNCC) Black founders, presented a paper protesting the inferior status of women in the organization. Women typed, filed, telephoned, and canvassed while men formulated strategies, made decisions, led meetings, and delivered speeches. "The only position for women in SNCC," responded Black leader Stokley Carmichael, "is prone." At the 1966 Students for a Democratic Society (SDS) convention, women, voicing the same concerns, presented a women's liberation plank. One observer later wrote that they were "pelted with tomatoes and thrown out of the convention." At a 1968 anti-Vietnam march in Washington, D.C., 5,000 women expressed their disillusionment with women's role in antiwar organizations by symbolically burying "traditional womanhood" at Arlington National Cemetery. In 1969, women working for the alternative press presented a resolution to the Underground Press Syndicate conference calling for the "elimination of male supremacy and chauvinism" in the contents of antiwar and counterculture newspapers.

Throughout the late 1960s, women were not only protesting within New Left groups, they were splitting off to establish their own organizations. The National Organization of Women (NOW) was founded in 1966, and feminist groups were established in at least 40 cities during 1968 and 1969. In 1968 five distinctly feminist publications were being issued, including the movement's first national newsletter. *The Voice of the Women's Liberation Movement*, founded by a coalition of Chicago women's groups, acted as a bulletin board for the emerging movement. That year also saw the publication of

NOW's first regular periodical, *NOW Acts*. Like the NOW national newsletter still being published today, the monthly discussed employment, legislation, court decisions, and women's treatment by the conventional press, in addition to highlighting special concerns like child care, sexual harassment, and rape. *Lilith*, a Seattle-based feminist magazine, and *No More Fun and Games*, a strident yet scholarly Boston publication, also began publishing in 1968. "You can't have a revolution without a press," wrote the editors of a feminist newsletter published in Pittsburgh the next year.

As the new decade began, feminist newsletters and newspapers proliferated. In 1970 alone, 73 different newsletters were started, about a quarter of them affiliated with state or regional NOW chapters. From San Diego came *Battle Acts*, a newspaper devoted to working-class women. From Milwaukee came *St. Joan's*, a feminist quarterly for Catholics. In Washington, D.C. a voluntary collective began publishing *Off Our Backs*. Papers flourished in major cities from New York to Los Angeles and in college towns from Iowa City to Eugene. Some were devoted to special groups within the women's movement—blacks, Chicanas, lesbians—others concentrated on literary, philosophic, and political fare. Most covered marches, speeches, legislative action, and court decisions. Many contained journalism that was both personal and angry.

"I used to lie in bed beside my husband . . . and wish I had the courage to bash in his head with a frying pan," wrote one woman. "Stay single," advised another. Other writers angrily shared their experiences with job discrimination and harassment. Some graphically described rapes and abortions. Politically, feminist journals ranged from moderate publications that called for government-subsidized child care to radical papers that supported the lesbian separatist movement. Almost two-thirds were run by collectives. None was headed by a male editor.

By the summer of 1972 when *Ms.* published its first regular issue, third-wave feminists had produced more than 500 newsletters, newspapers, magazines, and quarterly journals. The small editorial board of *Ms.* took what they considered the best features of the feminist press and combined them with slick paper, color photography, and sophisticated graphics. They wanted their magazine to be "serious, outrageous, satisfying, intimate, global, compassionate and as full of change as women's lives really are." The magazine combined hard-hitting articles with legislative news briefs, profiles of working women, self-help articles, and feminist poetry and fiction. Undoubtedly the publication's most discernible impact was popularizing the title "Ms." as a way of referring to women without supplying information on their marital status. Beyond that, *Ms.* reached women not affiliated with feminist groups, helping to expand feminist consciousness and set the stage for the feminism of the 1980s.

FEMINISM IN THE 1980s

Feminist filmmakers began producing documentaries of women's lives and women's issues. Feminist musicians formed their own bands and their own recording and distributing companies. Women started their own book publishing companies and advertising agencies. In one sense, feminism of the 1980s was expanding.

But in another important way, it was narrowing both its focus and its aim. By the early 1980s, the national feminist movement was devoting most of its resources to a single issue: passage of the Equal Rights Amendment. Many of the new feminist journals of the decade were designed to reach a select group of upwardly mobile professional women. *Working Woman* told its readers "how to play hardball in the corporate world" and "how to play golf to make contacts." *Savvy* discussed corporate etiquette and instructed its readers on playing the stock market. *Working Mother* discussed not how to balance commitments but how to get a divorce and apply for a home mortgage. At the same time, the 1980 census showed that most working women (who now numbered 53% of the adult female population) were still segregated in dead-end, female-only jobs. The new feminist ethic with its attention to dressing for success and moving up the corporate ladder was both ahead of its time and elitist. Perhaps most significantly, it appeard to be telling women that the only way to achieve full equality was to act like men.

FEMINIST VICTORIES AND THE PRESS

Unlike their nineteenth-century sisters, today's women can vote, hold political office, own businesses and property, attend universities, and pursue almost any career they choose. Women are still excluded from management and top decision-making positions in almost every field, and working women with the same demographic characteristics as men earn 45 cents to the man's dollar, but the 150-year-old feminist movement has led to many significant victories. The feminist press—along with women's organizations, lobbying efforts, and public action—has been at the core of these victories.

It is impossible to prove a direct cause-effect link between feminist journalism and the success of the women's movement, but several things are clear. Without the feminist press a host of dissident ideas—from women's political equality to reproductive freedom—would not have received a public forum. The nineteenth-century conventional press, wrote national suffrage leaders, regularly referred to those fighting for political equality as "hyenas, cats, crowing hens, bold wantons, unsexed females and dangerous homewreckers." When they weren't ridiculing women's efforts, mainstream newspapers and magazines of the nineteenth century simply ignored the feminist movement. A vast body of research in the twentieth century shows that the modern-day conventional media have also taken the easy route of ridicule (the 1960s "bra burners") and stereotype (pushy, loud-mouthed, asexual women like television's "Maude"). But for the most part, even during the height of activism in the late 1960s, the conventional press has ignored the women's movement. With little access to the mainstream press of their day, feminists depended on their own publications to speak for themselves and their cause.

In addition to acting as forums for ideas, the feminist press enhanced intramovement communication and aided in internal organization. Especially in the nineteenth century, when national communications and transportation networks were not yet developed, feminists from New England to the Northwest were linked through the pages of their newspapers and periodicals. Feminist publications helped boost the morale of their readers, particularly during the long fight for women's enfranchisement and the ongoing battle for the passage of the ERA. From *Lily* in the 1840s to *Ms.* in the 1980s, feminist periodicals have instructed, propagandized, and served as outlets for the hopes and frustrations of those women who dared to go against the grain.

REFERENCES

The following material aided in the preparation of this chapter and is suggested for further reading:

Bennion, Sherilyn Cox. "The New Northwest and Woman's Exponent: Early Voices for Suffrage." Journalism Quarterly, 54, (Summer 1977), pp. 286-292.

Catt, Carrie Chapman and Shuler, Nettie Rogers. Woman Suffrage and Politics. New York: Charles Scribner's Sons, 1923.

Chafe, William H. The American Woman: Her Changing Social, Economic and Political Roles, 1920-1970. New York: Oxford University Press, 1972.

Chafe, William H. Woman and Equality. New York: Oxford University Press, 1977.

Flexner, Eleanor. Century of Struggle: The Woman's Rights Movement in the United States. New York: Atheneum, 1973.

Friedan, Betty. The Feminine Mystique. New York: W. W. Norton, 1963.

Hymowitz, Carol and Weissman, Michaele. A History of Women in America. New York: Bantam, 1978.

Kessler, Lauren. "A Siege of the Citadels: A Search for a Public Forum for the Ideas of Oregon Woman Suffrage." Oregon Historical Quarterly, 84, (Summer 1983), pp. 117-149.

Kraditor, Aileen S. Ideas of the Woman Suffrage Movement 1890-1920. New York: Columbia University Press, 1965.

Lemons, J. Stanley. The Woman Citizen: Social Feminism in the 1920s. Urbana: University of Illinois Press, 1973.

Marzolf, Marion. Up From the Footnote: A History of Women Journalists. New York: Hastings House, 1977.

Mather, Ann. "A History of Feminist Periodicals." Journalism History, 1, (Autumn 1974), pp. 82-85; 1, (Winter 1974-1975), pp. 108-111; 2, (Spring 1975), pp. 19-23+.

O'Neill, William. Everyone Was Brave: A History of Feminism in America. New York: Quadrangle, 1969.

Reed, James. From Private Vice to Public Virtue: The Birth Control Movement and American Society Since 1830. New York: Basic Books, 1978.

Sinclair, Andrew. Emancipation of the American Woman. New York: Harper & Row, 1965.

Stanton, Elizabeth Cady. The History of Woman Suffrage, Vols. I-III, Rochester, NY, 1881-1886; Vol. IV. Rochester, NY, 1902; Vols. V-VI, New York, 1922.

5

STRANGERS IN A STRANGE LAND

We are come to rest and push our roots more deeply by the year. But we cannot push away the heritage of having been once all strangers in the land.

—Oscar Handlin

America is a land of immigrants. More patchwork quilt than melting pot, the United States has been, and is, home to dozens of distinct national groups. First came the religious dissidents: the English, the German and Scandinavian Quakers, and a number of northern European sects. Then came the land-hungry German and Scandinavian peasants. Next to arrive were the Irish escaping the 1846 potato famine and the Germans and Slavs fleeing the 1848 revolution. In the 1880s Italian and Slavic peasants looking to better their lot and eastern European Jews escaping Russian pograms arrived on America's shores. In the early twentieth century, the war in Europe and the political instability of their homelands—as well as the promise of a better economic future—brought millions of immigrants to the New World. Between 1901 and 1920, 3.25 million Italians, 1.5 million Poles, 1 million Germans, and hundreds of thousands of Greeks, Japanese, French, Scandinavians, Dutch, and Bohemians came to the United States. Most arrived penniless, friendless, and unable to speak or read the language of their adopted homeland.

Yet more than those already settled in the New World, foreign-speaking immigrants needed basic information. How does one find a job? Where does one live? How do American economic, political, and educational systems work? To the peasant immigrants of the late nineteenth and early twentieth centuries, accustomed to the close-knit village, a direct relationship to the land and a life encircled by extended families, the New World was an alien environment. Not just the language but the entire culture left them feeling isolated and estranged. They desperately needed information to help them understand this new culture and how to live in it. They hungered for news about the countries and the villages they left behind.

The existing English-language press did not suit their needs. First, of course, it was written in a language they did not yet understand. But even those few who could read English, or those who quickly learned, found the conventional press irrelevant to their situation. Newspapers were written for the already acclimated "older immigrants"—the American middle class—who had very different informational needs than the new immigrants. What these new immigrants needed, in addition to their religious organizations and self-help societies, was a press of their own.

This they produced in great profusion—in dozens of different languages, in major urban centers as well as rural outposts—from the early eighteenth century to the present. Since colonial times, the foreign-language press has existed alongside the dominant English-language press supplying information, opinion, and entertainment to millions of immigrants.

The foreign-language press began somewhat inauspiciously in 1732 when journalist-inventor-diplomat Ben Franklin began publishing the *Philadelphische Zeitung*. Pennsylvania was home to a number of early German immigrants, most of whom apparently had little regard for Franklin's newspaper, which was written in fractured German by a French printer in Franklin's employ. After only a few issues the paper ceased publication. Seven years later, German immigrant printer Christopher Sauer started a more successful weekly in Pennsylvania, and throughout the eighteenth century the German-language press proliferated. During the revolutionary war period, five reasonably successful German newspapers were being published in Pennsylvania, and in the last few decades of the eighteenth century Germans published 39 newspapers in the colonies.

The French also established their own press in the eighteenth century. *Le Courier de Boston*, which published weekly for six months during 1789, was their first effort. Although Native Americans and the Spanish-speaking people of the Southwest could hardly be considered immigrants (the Anglo pioneers who encroached on their land were the immigrants), they constitute distinct non-English-language communities that early on felt a need for a press of their own. In 1828 the Cherokee Nation established the first Native American newspaper, the *Cherokee Phoenix,* in Georgia. With the publication of *El Misisipi* in 1808, Spanish-speaking people established their own journalistic tradition. The Scandinavians, another early immigrant group, began publishing their own journals in the mid-1840s.

But prior to the massive wave of immigration in the 1880s, most of the foreign-language press, like the majority of the foreign-language population, was German. Out of 822 foreign language newspapers and magazines being published in 1885, 653 of them—79%—were German. Although the German press continued to account for more than half the total foreign-language publications in the United States until 1913, its dominance lessened as other immigrant groups arrived in the New World. By the turn of the century, Bohemians were publishing 44 journals, Poles 41, Italians 36. From 1884 to 1920 immigrants started a total of 3,444 new publications (3,186 did not last), of which only 35% were German language. In the first two decades of the twentieth century, as Italians, Poles, Greeks, and Japanese immigrated in record numbers, the number and variety of their publications increased proportionately. In 1920, *Literary Digest* reported that 1,500 foreign-language newspapers and magazines with an aggregate circulation of 8 million were being printed in 33 languages in every state of the union. Wrote University of Chicago sociologist Robert Park in his 1922 study of the immigrant press: "In the city of New York . . . there is, so far as can be learned, no language group so insignificant that it does not maintain a printing press and publish some sort of periodical." Indeed, New York City in 1920 supported Italian, German, Polish, Spanish, and Jewish newspapers, each with circulations in excess of 100,000, as well as 141 other foreign-language journals.

WHY THE FOREIGN-LANGUAGE PRESS EMERGED

Clearly, establishing and maintaining their own newspapers and magazines was a top priority for dozens of foreign-language-speaking national groups. Park, who studied the foreign-language press as part of a multi-volume study on

Americanization, believed that the immigrant press thrived in the New World because many of these national groups had not been permitted to read, publish, or be educated in their own language in Europe. The Lithuanians, Ukranians, and Slovaks, for example, had been denied use of their native tongues as their countries were Russified, Polonized, Magyarized, and Germanized. By the mid-1800s, Lithuania was so completely Polonized that native speech ceased to be the language of the literate classes. Not until 1883 was a Lithuanian magazine published in Lithuania; but between 1834 and 1895 at least 34 Lithuanian periodicals were published in the United States. By 1920, there were more Slovak papers in the United States than there were in Hungary.

Park argues that for the "oppressed and dependent nationalities of Europe" the social and economic unrest of the nineteenth century had gradually focused on the struggle to raise the native peasant languages to the language of the schools and the press. In America, writes Park, "the intellectual representative of a suppressed race is . . . given free hand to do what was prohibited at home: establish a press in his mother tongue." It should be remembered that Park was writing during the extraordinarily patriotic years following World War I. He neglected to mention that America did not always welcome immigrants with open arms, nor that some foreign-language newspapers were suppressed during World War I. But the inhibition of some peasant languages in Europe is a fact, and it may very well have contributed to the growth of some foreign-language newspapers in the New World.

But there were more potent reasons for the development and proliferation of the foreign-language press. The newly arrived millions needed information to help them learn about and adjust to life in America. They and many of the immigrants who came before them yearned for news of their native countries. Their own foreign-language press could serve both purposes: promoting Americanization while preserving feelings of ethnicity that caused, and still cause, Americans to argue about the place of the foreign-language press in the United States.

Behind this argument lies the "melting pot" imperative: Immigrants, regardless of their ethnic backgrounds, should learn quickly to talk and behave as Americans. To preserve one's ethnic heritage was seen as heresy. Why come to America if not to become an American? Especially during times of societal change, when millions of immigrants landed on U.S. shores between the 1880s and the early twentieth century, the already settled and assimilated immigrants ("Americans") pushed for the Americanization of the new immigrants. Those who identified strongly with America as a melting pot were concerned about the foreign-language press: Would it aid in the Americanization process, or would it retard Americanization by helping to preserve ethnicity?

Some viewed the foreign-language press as an impediment. It helped isolate immigrants from American society by perpetuating the use of their native languages and supporting their ethnic traditions. It helped maintain unity among members of the national group and helped preserve nationalistic feelings, thus insulating them from the wider society. By offering news of their native countries, the press promoted identification with the Old World instead of the New. In short, the foreign-language press preserved feelings of separateness.

But others argued that the foreign-language press was an important aid to assimilation. "Reading a foreign language newspaper was a step in the Americanization of the immigrant," wrote Pulitzer prize-winning historian Oscar Handlin in 1951. "It helped him interpret the issues and events of the day and provided him with the information he needed to operate in the community and the larger society he had entered." By publishing American news, the foreign press helped immigrants become familiar with U.S. events, ideas, and customs. It educated them on the American point of view and helped them understand and respect American institutions. Not only did this aid in the immigrants' adjustment, it stimulated interest in their adopted homeland.

The foreign-language press was, said some, an educational agency without equal. It provided immigrants with a political education while, by its very existence, encouraging literacy. Newspapers publicized night school and citizenship and English classes. Some regularly published English lessons and columns on American history. Foreign-language newspapers, wrote one student of the Polish press, acted as "advertisements for the American way of life, American . . . businesses, organizations, entertainment." And of course there was the actual advertising of American products. A pamphlet circulated in 1919 called national advertising "the great Americanizer" because it "tells the story of American business, pluck, enterprise and achievement." The circular urged American businesses to "combine business and patriotism" by advertising in the foreign-language press.

From the melting pot point of view, the foreign-language press was both an accelerator and a brake to Americanization. Clearly, it did introduce immigrants to American politics, culture, and society. But it also enabled them to preserve common traditions and common speech. These purposes, however, may not have been as contradictory as they seemed. By speaking to them in their own language and sustaining a sense of group identity, the foreign-language press may have helped immigrants overcome severe culture shock. By lessening their feeling of dislocation the press may have helped accelerate the adjustment process.

COMPLEXITY AND CHANGE

But to speak of foreign-language journalism as a monolith oversimplifies and distorts the purposes and often changing functions of the press. The most obvious difference among the thousands of foreign-language journals—the languages in which they were printed—only begins to tell the story of their diversity. Because the growth of the various foreign-language journals mirrored immigration patterns, and because these patterns changed, the immigrant press itself changed. The press that was established prior to 1870 served a different kind of immigrant than the press established after 1870. Immigrants prior to 1870 were mostly northern Europeans. The British, Dutch, Scandinavians, and French were early settlers. In the 1840s the German and Irish came in great numbers. Between 1861 and 1870 45% of all immigrants were either British or Irish. But by 1891-1900, British and Irish comprised only 18% of all immigrants, while southern Europeans accounted for 50%. During the first decade of the twentieth century, with more than a million immigrants arriving each year, Italians, Russians, and Austro-Hungarians accounted for more than three-quarters of the total number of immigrants.

Not only were there immigrants from different countries, they also came to America for different reasons and settled in different parts of the country. The newspapers and periodicals they established reflected these differences. The pre-1870 northern European immigrants were, in general, political or religious dissidents. Many came to the New World in order to settle the land. Some came with money; others came knowing they could count on the assistance of family or friends who preceded them. Germans established enclaves in Pennsylvania, Ohio, and Wisconsin. Scandinavians settled in Minnesota and the Dakotas. Except for the Irish during the 1840s, many of whom came to the New World destitute and were forced to settle in the port cities they landed in, the pre-1870 immigrants tended to move to rural areas. The press they established was provincial press concerned with rural life, farming, religion, and preserving the memories of the villages or regions from which the immigrants came. Like the community newspapers of today, these rural journals were chatty weeklies limited in scope to the small geographical area in which they existed.

The post-1870 immigrants were mainly southern and eastern Europeans who came to America not as dissidents but as refugees. As landless peasants, they arrived in New York City, the terminus for the overwhelming majority of steamships from Europe, often with little more than a bundle of clothing. Those who came with savings found it was much easier to get work than land in post-Civil War America. Of necessity, most settled where they landed—New York. Some, like the Poles and Slavs, found employment in the industrial centers of the East and Midwest. These new immigrants were city dwellers or industrial migrants, and they created and supported an urban, cosmopolitan press. By 1920 more than half the newspapers serving these post-1870 immigrants were being published in the nation's ten largest cities.

Because of the pace of urban life, these newspapers tended to be dailies. They were filled with news of the city and, like the cities' English-language press, they maintained an interest in world affairs and politics. Because the cost of operating a foreign-language metropolitan daily was far greater than that of publishing a rural weekly, urban dailies needed wide circulation. This meant that papers tried to appeal to an entire immigrant group (Italians, for example) rather than the smaller, provincial groups (Sicilians, Calabrians) to which the rural papers appealed.

But categorizing the foreign language press according to the rural pre-1870 immigrants and their provincial weeklies and the post-1870 urban immigrants and their metropolitan dailies is still an oversimplification. Some groups, like the Germans, were both urban and rural. Even those groups that maintained a consistent lifestyle went through various stages of accommodation and assimilation. As the group changed, its newspapers and magazines changed to fulfill new needs. Additionally, the foreign-language press did not exist in a vacuum. Upheavals in American society—the growing rift between labor and business, economic depression, war—affected its content, purpose, and direction. The German press is a good illustration of the complexity of foreign-language journalism in America.

THE GERMAN-LANGUAGE PRESS

As one of the earliest immigrant groups, the Germans established the first foreign-language newspapers in America, and throughout the colonial and revolutionary war periods their press gained momentum. Pennsylvania, home to the majority of German-speaking people, was the site of most of these early papers. Thirty-eight were published there before the end of the eighteenth century. Like most of the English-language journals of the time, these papers were weeklies that, because of the difficulty of colonial communication, made liberal use of previously published material. They were provincial newspapers not only because they were concerned with rural life but also because they reflected regional and sectarian differences among the German immigrant groups in the New World.

Many of the papers were published in towns settled by immigrants from one distinct region of Germany—Westphalia, the Rhine Valley, Alsace-Lorraine—and were printed in the local dialect. Many of the founders of these early newspapers were, like the provincial groups they wrote for, religious dissidents who wanted to establish isolated enclaves in the New World in order to practice their beliefs freely. Thus the papers contained a good deal of religious matter. But despite its provincial nature, the early German-language press took a lively interest in politics, focusing on colonial as well as European activities. In fact, it has been said that the first news of the adoption of the Declaration of Independence was printed in a German-language newspaper on July 5, 1776.

By the early decades of the nineteenth century, German immigrants were establishing settlements and starting newspapers in St. Louis, Cincinnati, and other midwestern towns. As these frontier settlements grew throughout the 1800s, newspapers like the St. Louis *Westlich Post*—where later Joseph Pulitzer was to get his start in journalism—the Cincinnati *Volksblatt,* and the (Chicago) *Illinois Stass-Zeitung* also grew. As the settlements became urban centers, the press became cosmopolitan.

New Immigrants of the Nineteenth Century

Beginning the 1840s, a portion of the German-language press began to reflect a new kind of German immigrant, the restless and frustrated intellectual who migrated to the New World in the years leading up to and following the Revolution of 1848. These new immigrants were politically adventurous—some were overtly radical—and they moved to America's fast-growing cities, there establishing outspoken newspapers. Dailies in Baltimore, Cleveland, Milwaukee, and Detroit were evidence of this cosmopolitan press. Perhaps because these papers were both political and nationalistic, they—and their readers—became targets of a chauvinistic organization called the Native American Party. Established in 1848 and later called the Know-Nothing Party, this group decried the continuing influx of Europeans. Capitalizing on the instinctive fear of foreigners, the party proposed to return America to "Americans." In Baltimore, home of the daily *Der Deutsche Correspondent,* organized gangs armed with carpenter's awls jabbed voters at the polls who failed to give the secret password. Bands of party hoodlums roamed the streets in German neighborhoods firing pistols to intimidate residents. Editors were threatened. In St. Louis, where the sizable German population supported the *Westlich Post,* party members instigated street battles. This was the first, but hardly the last, instance of American intolerance of German-Americans and their press.

The pattern of German immigration shows peaks in 1854, 1873, and 1882 followed by a steady decrease thereafter, and the growth of the German-language press mirrors this pattern. From the 1850s through the 1880s, Germans established new dailies in Cleveland, Milwaukee, Detroit, St. Louis, and Chicago and strong weeklies in these and other midwestern towns. A few of these were politically radical journals that espoused anarchism and syndicalism (a form of trade unionism). Neither was a popular cause at the time, and the radical newspapers and their editors became even less popular when an anarchist rally turned into the bloody Haymarket Riot in 1886. Several German-language newspaper editors were jailed and two were executed because they allegedly instigated and incited the riot. But most German-language publications were not anarchist organs. The press continued to grow throughout the late nineteenth century. At one point in the 1890s, St. Louis supported 21 different German-language publications, and Germans published 82 daily newspapers in the New World. At its all-time high in 1893, the German-language press numbered 796 publications, including both cosmopolitan and provincial journals. But by the end of World War I, only 276 German-language publications remained, including 26 dailies.

World War I and Decline

Both the decrease in immigration and the process of assimilation caused some of this sharp decline. As older German immigrants learned English and acclimated themselves to American society, they increasingly turned to English-language dailies for their news. And with fewer new immigrants arriving, the German-language press attracted fewer new readers. But the main cause of the sharp decline in the early twentieth century was the war itself. Even prior to America's entrance into the European war, the U.S. government and most of the conventional English-language newspapers were sympathetic to Britain and hostile to Germany. But for the 10 million people who listed Germany as their country of origin (along with millions of Slavs and Austro-Hungarians) the war presented a difficult choice. Caught between their new loyalty to the United States and their old loyalty to the Fatherland, German immigrants found themselves in a precarious position that worsened as the U.S. commitment to the Allies grew.

The German-language press was also caught in a dilemma. The editors wanted to reflect the sentiments of their readers while avoiding offending the U.S. government. Sometimes this meant that even an outspokenly pro-German newspaper would decorate its front page with American flags, publish the words to the "Star Spangled Banner," and offer free advertising space to patriotic causes. Sometimes it meant that a newspaper wavered weekly—even daily—between supporting the Central Powers and supporting U.S. policy. Often it meant that German-language newspapers editorially encouraged pacifism and noninterventionism. Some German newspaper editors took pains to explain their "Americanizing" function and put their ties to Germany in perspective. Printed across the top of the front page in a 1916 issue of *Der Deutsche Correspondent* was this statement of policy:

> To acquaint the Germans newly arrived in this country with the social and political conditions in the United States; to familiarize them with their duties towards their adopted country and with the rights conferred upon them by the Constitution; to keep alive and foster their love for German social life and song; ... to impress their children with the value of cultivating interest in the language of their fathers—this was the purpose which inspired the founding of the German Correspondent ... and this will remain its purpose.

The *Correspondent*, as well as other German-language newspapers of the era, stressed not political but social and cultural ties to Germany.

Like many of the German-language papers, the *Correspondent* had been elated by German victories in the early years of the war. But after the United States declared war on Germany, the *Correspondent* advised its readers to remember their oath of loyalty to America. "Keep in mind that while Germany is the land of our fathers, this is the land of our children and our children's children," said a 1917 editorial. Nevertheless, the *Correspondent* was accused of being openly pro-German, and to avoid government intervention it suspended publication in 1918, resuming after the war. Ten years later, the *Correspondent* still found it necessary to counter American suspicion of the German-language press. A 1928 editorial stated:

> [*The Correspondent*], as all papers in the United States in the German language are not German papers, but American papers printed in the German language. They represent American interests as completely as the papers printed in the English language. They educate the Germans who come to this country to become good and loyal American citizens.

Prior to America's entrance in the war, many German papers expounded on the German point of view while calling for U.S. neutrality. When the United States joined the war, most of the relatively few German-language publications that had openly supported the Fatherland turned to preaching pacifism. A handful continued to denounce U.S. policy. But even for those publications supporting the war, the going was rough. Said the man who edited the New York *Staas-Zeitung* during World War I:

> German-Americans were persecuted in World War I, afraid to be seen with a German-language newspaper. If delivered to an apartment building and others saw it, there was trouble. We lost nearly half our circulation this way.

Just the act of reading German while America was at war with Germany was considered by some to be proof of disloyalty.

Government Control

Concerned with what the foreign press was telling its readers, the U.S. government made its first serious attempt to control the immigrant press during World War I. Not surprisingly, German-language periodicals were a major target. Faced with dissension—or at least not wholehearted support—from the German-American population as well as powerful propaganda from the Central Powers, the American government decided to fight the war with words as well as guns.

A week after the declaration of war, President Woodrow Wilson created the Committee on Public Information to coordinate government propaganda efforts and act as the government's liaison with newspapers. Headed by newspaperman George Creel, the committee soon established a subgroup called the Division of Work Among the Foreign Born. The division translated pro-United States, prowar articles into 14 different languages and functioned as a press service, disseminating the material to more than 700 foreign-language newspapers. At one point in 1917, the government contemplated imposing a licensing fee on all foreign-language publications. Rear Admiral Cooper F. Goodrich suggested a one cent per-copy tax for daily newspapers and a 10 cent per-issue tax for monthly publications on the theory that the foreign language press was a "luxury" for those who "remaining in our midst, are unwilling to take the trouble to learn English." Goodrich may or may not have known what foreign-language editors knew quite well: Many readers of foreign publications were perfectly capable of reading English but chose to read journals in their own language because they could gain access to news and information not contained in English-language publications. Clearly, Goodrich's plan was designed as a punishment for foreign-language journals and would indeed have caused financial hardship—and closure of many smaller publication—had it been enacted.

What the government did enact, however, was a much more powerful curb on free expression in the foreign-language press than the tax plan could ever have been. The Espionage Act of June 15, 1917 created a legal mechanism for suppressing antiwar, anti-American or anti-Allies sentiments. During wartime, anyone who promoted the success of enemies of the United States, caused or attempted to cause insubordination, disloyalty, or refusal of military duty, or obstructed recruitment could be punished by up to 20 years' imprisonment and a $10,000 fine. A special section of the act empowered the Postmaster General to declare unmailable newspapers, periodicals, or any other published matter if they violated provisions of the act. During the first year of the Espionage Act, almost 80 publications lost their mailing privileges or retained them only by agreeing to banish all articles about the war from their pages. Some of these publications were German-language papers; others were socialist publications preaching pacifism and noninterventionism.

Four months later, the government increased its control of German and other foreign-language publications by passing the Trading with the Enemy Act. This authorized censorship of all communication in or out of the United States and empowered the Post Office to demand translations of all articles published in a foreign language. In May 1918, the Sedition Act broadened the Espionage Act by making it a crime to publish disloyal or scurrilous articles about the country, the flag, the constitution, or the military. In response to government suppression, anti-German hysteria, and the decrease in the number of German immigrants, the German-language press declined rapidly during the war years.

World War II to the Present

By the late 1930s, the German press numbered a mere 178 publications, only a dozen of them dailies. The Americanized immigrants and their American-born children were reading English-language dailies for their news. To a great extent, the German-language press had returned to its earlier provincial status, publishing cultural and religious news its readers could not get elsewhere. Prior to Pearl Harbor and the United States' entry into World War II, perhaps a dozen German-language newspapers were openly pro-Nazi, including weeklies on both coasts, the New York *Neue Volkszeitung,* and the Portland *Nachrichten.* Papers in Schenectady, Miami, Dayton, and Omaha were violently anti-Nazi. But the majority of German-language papers were indifferent, noncommittal, or divided. Two of the oldest and most respected newspapers—the New York *Staas-Zeitung* and the Rochester *Abenpost*—were embarrassed and disturbed by the Nazi development in Germany. Like many other German-language publications, they tried to avoid the issue of Nazism while maintaining their traditionally anti-British posture and calling for U.S. isolationism. After Pearl Harbor the few pro-Nazi publications dropped out of sight, and the German-language press as a whole kept a low profile.

Nevertheless, it was a difficult time for the German (and the Italian and Japanese) press. Censorship was a factor, but just as important was America's suspicion and hatred of all things related to the Axis powers. In 1942 Army officials were reportedly in favor of suspending all German, Italian, and Japanese publications. Some voluntarily suspended publication to avoid government interference; some shifted their support to American war efforts; others omitted all news of the war; a few began to publish English-language editions, apparently to show their loyalty. Beyond the ideological problems, the war had deep repercussions for German-language and other foreign-language publications. With consumer products scarce or rationed, advertising income diminished. Any financial support received from home governments stopped, as did the flow of newspapers and magazines from the old country that had provided some reprint material. In the postwar years and into the late twentieth century, the German-language press continued its decline until, in 1980, only two German-language dailies were being published.

The history of the German-language press illustrates several important characteristics of the foreign-language press as a whole. First, the type of immigrant has an effect on the kind of journalism that develops. Immigrants who move to rural outposts or establish isolated enclaves are generally served by provincial publications. Urban or migrant industrial immigrants support a cosmopolitan press—at least for a while. One immigrant group can contain both rural and urban populations simultaneously or at different times and thus can support both provincial and cosmopolitan publications. Second, the development of the foreign-language press mirrors immigration patterns. A few years after a peak in immigration, the press grows accordingly to serve the needs of the new immigrants. As immigration slackens and as older immigrants become Americanized, the cosmopolitan press wanes and the provincial press remains as a sentimental reminder of Old World culture. Third, the foreign-language press exists within the context of American society and is affected by the politics, economics, and social stresses of the culture within which it functions.

OTHER FOREIGN-LANGUAGE JOURNALISM

The Scandinavian Press

Although German publications dominated the foreign-language press throughout the eighteenth, nineteenth, and early twentieth centuries, they were by no means the only important journalistic efforts by immigrants. Scandinavian immigrants and settlers supported a large and varied press, which, in terms of number of publications, ranked second to the German press. For the most part, the Scandinavians were "settler" immigrants who moved to farming communites in the Midwest. Their journals, like the early German publications, were rural weeklies that concentrated on religious and cultural discussions. In his 1922 study of the immigrant press, sociologist Robert Park reported that one-third of all the Norwegian journals ever published in the United States were distinctly religious. It was not until 19 years after the founding of the first Scandinavian newspaper—the short-lived *Scandinavia* in 1847—that the New World saw the first successful attempt at a secular Scandinavian newspaper. Despite its ties to the Church, the Scandinavian press grew to include a wide variety of journalism: general newspapers, ethnic and community newspapers, partisan organs, farmers' magazines, women's magazines, humor and literary journals, and at least ten socialist and labor publications. But throughout the years, it remained primarily a weekly or monthly press, reflecting the rural settlement of the Scandinavians.

During the mid- and late nineteenth century, the Scandinavian press grew rapidly as the immigration from Norway, Denmark, and Sweden reached record numbers. Almost a half-million Danes emigrated before the turn of the century, and by 1900 Swedish immigrants in the United States numbered one-quarter of the population of Sweden. The Scandinavian press as a whole jumped from 53 publications in 1884 to 135 in 1894. Probably more than 700 different Scandinavian newspapers and periodicals lived and died during the late nineteenth and early twentieth centuries.

In her study of Danish-language journalism, University of Michigan journalism educator Marion Marzolf contends that the press acted mostly as an accelerator in the assimilation process. By giving the immigrants information they needed to function in the new society, by promoting citizenship and active participation in public affairs, and by lessening culture shock, the Scandinavian journals hastened the Americanization of their readers. Wrote Scandinavian editor and publisher Hans Matson, who later became Minnesota's Secretary of State: "My aim . . . was mainly to instruct and educate my countrymen in such matters as might promote their well-being and make them good American citizens." As Scandinavians became "good American citizens," their journals changed to suit new needs. A number became English-language journals directed to those of Scandinavian ancestry.

The Spanish-Language Press

By the end of the nineteenth century, the Spanish-language press ranked third in number of publications among foreign-language groups. As would be expected, the earliest journals began in two areas heavily populated by Spanish-speaking people. New Orleans, a seaport that actively traded with Latin America, was the site of the first Spanish-language newspaper, *El Misisipi* (1808). Throughout the early nineteenth century, the city supported a number of Spanish-language and bilingual publications. The other site of early Spanish-language journalism, the area that later became Texas, New Mexico, and Arizona, was owned by Mexico until 1848. The Spanish-speaking people who lived there could hardly be called immigrants, but their journalistic efforts were certainly part of the foreign-language press. At least six newspapers were published in this territory before the Yankee conquest.

Thoughout the nineteenth century, the Southwest continued to be the hub of Spanish-language journalism, with more than 130 different newspapers published prior to 1900. But many of these newspapers were owned and operated by Anglos who received government subsidies for printing bilingual or Spanish-language editions. One study of New Mexico journalism during this period found that only 12% of the journalists working for Spanish or bilingual newspapers were themselves Spanish-Americans. Although many of these nineteenth century newspapers were moderate in tone, some decried Yankee oppression, violence, and discrimination and others called for improved educational and job opportunities for Spanish-speaking people. Because of their unique position as displaced natives rather than immigrants, the Spanish-speaking people of the Southwest and California created and supported newspapers calling for strong cultural identity rather than Americanization. One Los Angeles weekly argued that the ability to speak Spanish was essential to the well-being of the

Chicano community. A Texas newspaper attacked those who denied their Mexican roots.

Into the twentieth century, California and the Southwest continued to support the bulk of Spanish-language journalism. The Chicano movement, sparked by the California grape-worker's strike in the 1960s, spurred radical journalism like *La Raza* and a half-dozen newspapers in Texas. But not all Mexican-Americans remained in the Southwest, and when they migrated to cities throughout the Midwest, their newspapers soon followed, Additionally, not all Spanish-speaking people had Mexican ancestry. Puerto Ricans, Cubans, and Latin Americans migrated to the United States throughout the late nineteenth and twentieth centuries, many of them settling in New York City and Miami. In fact, the first Spanish-language daily, *La Prensa,* was published in New York in 1912. In 1980, Spanish-language dailies were being published in Los Angeles, Miami, New York City, Laredo, and El Paso.

The Yiddish Press

Jewish or Yiddish journalism, although relatively small in number of publications, has included some of the largest-circulation dailies of any foreign-language press and is one of the best examples of cosmopolitan journalism by an immigrant group. The Yiddish press, which began with the 1872 publication of the weekly *Judische Post,* grew slowly and steadily throughout the late nineteenth and early twentieth centuries. Jews from Eastern Europe and Russian, escaping discrimination and pogroms, flocked to the New World by the millions. Most of the immigrants, both peasants and intellectuals, settled where they landed, New York City, and in 1885 the first Jewish daily was published in that city. Both the increase in Jewish immigration and the concentration of Jews in urban centers were reflected in the growth of their daily press. In 1885, their one daily newspaper reached 3,750 readers. By 1915, five dailies were reaching a combined circulation of more than half a million.

The Yiddish press had an enormous educational impact on its audience because, in essence, it created its own reading public. In Europe, Yiddish had not been the language of education or literature, thus most Jewish immigrants had never learned to read the language they used in conversation. Since only a handful of Jewish scholars read Hebrew, most of the Jewish papers in the New World were printed in Yiddish. The new immigrants used their publications first to learn how to read and then to learn how to adjust to their new environment. In the Yiddish press they found news of the city, the nation, and the world, articles on science, education, and theology as well as humor, fiction, and coverage of the arts. They depended on Yiddish papers for international news pertaining to Jews, news to which the English-language dailies paid little attention. But they also found lengthy discussions of U.S. politics, labor unionism, and urban problems. Education, understanding American institutions, the responsibilities of citizenship, and participation in government were major topics in the Yiddish press.

In the 1920s, researcher Mordecai Soltes asked almost 400 readers of the New York City Yiddish press about themselves and their reading habits. He found that although more than 90% were foreign born, almost 80% of the readers had already become American citizens. Of those polled, 66% could, and did, read English-language newspapers. Only 14% could not read English. When he asked those who could read English why they continued reading the Yiddish press, 20% said they were attached to the language and did not want to see it die. Eighty percent said the Yiddish press offered them news about European and American Jewry they could not get in the English-language dailies. Although this study looked only at readers of the Yiddish press, its major finding is probably generalizable to the foreign-language press as a whole: Immigrants continued to support newspapers in their native tongue not because they could not read English but because their own press fulfilled unique cultural and informational needs.

The Japanese Press

Another immigrant group that supported a largely cosmo-politan press was the Japanese. More than 200,000 Japanese immigrants came to America during the first two decades of the twentieth century, increasing the Japanese-American population by more than 300%. In the same 20 years, immigrant editors started 24 new newspapers in the centers of greatest Japanese population, the cities of the West Coast. By 1922, Japanese were publishing 20 newspapers in Seattle, Los Angeles, and San Francisco, including two dailies each in San Francisco and Los Angeles. Serving not only the urban population but the agricultural settlements outside the cities, the papers included local, national, and international news as well as agricultural information and fiction. But their appeal to Japanese immigrants on the West Coast was probably more than the sum of their editorial content. In a country that was openly hostile to their presence, Japanese found a sense of community and a source of unity in their native-language publications.

In the early 1900s, anti-Japanese (and anti-Chinese) sentiment swelled along the West Coast. Concerned with the influx of cheap labor, West Coast politicians convinced President Theodore Roosevelt to restrict Japanese immigration. In 1907, Japan and the United States drew up a Gentlemen's Agreement in which Japan promised not to issue passports to laborers that would permit them to sail to the United States, and United States agreed not to adopt a formal Japanese exclusion act. The long-standing hostility toward the Japanese turned to hysteria after Pearl Harbor. Thousands of Japanese-Americans were herded into internment camps, and Japanese newspapers abruptly ceased publication. But in the postwar years, the urban dailies and weeklies were reborn. In 1980, Japanese-Americans supported four dailies—two in San Francisco, two in Los Angeles—and scores of weeklies.

Other Immigrant Groups

Dozens of other foreign-language groups produced hundreds of newspapers and periodicals, which helped them retain their cultural pride while aiding in the process of assimilation. Polish-Americans started more than 1,300 different newspapers and periodicals beginning with a Polish-language weekly in 1863. During the first two decades of the twentieth century, when almost 1.5 million Poles immigrated to America, 122 new publications were started. In the mid-1970s, Polish-Americans published 107 newspapers and magazines in 41 U.S. cities. In 1980, Polish dailies in New York, Chicago, and Detroit were still being published. Greeks began publishing journals in their native tongue in the late 1800s and, during their period of

greatest immigration, 1901-1920, started 29 new newspapers.
In 1950, five Greek dailies were being published. Other
national groups like the Chinese, Czechoslovakians, Lithuanians,
Russians, Armenians, and Arabs have all maintained their own
newspapers and periodicals.

THE IMMIGRANT PRESS PERSEVERES

The character and contents of foreign-language press papers
were an index of the interests, ambitions, and attitudes of the
people who read them. The gradual process of Americanization
was reflected in the lengthening columns of American news and
the space devoted to the immigrant groups' activities in the
New World. Advertising also reflected Americanization. The
newspapers of new immigrant groups were filled with advertising for immigrant-owned businesses and products related to
the culture of their homeland. As immigrant groups became
assimilated into American society, they began to patronize
American merchants and buy American products. Advertising in
these older immigrant journals reflected this change.

American society altered the lives, habits, language, and
customs of the immigrants. It also altered their newspapers.
Founded on the European tradition of the high-minded journal
of opinion, the foreign-language press discovered that to stay
alive it had to appeal to a broad spectrum of people. Competing
in urban markets meant increasing circulation and advertising.
To do this, many foreign-language newspapers in the twentieth
century became less ideological, less idealistic, and less
educational. They began to publish more news and less
opinion. They began to see themselves as forums for advertising. Like the successful English-language newspapers they
imitated, many foreign-language newspapers simplified their
language, paid more attention to police and crime news,
published human interest stories, and shied away from weighty
political discussions. The press, like its readers, became
Americanized.

It changed, but it persevered. Despite the slackening of
European immigration, despite the Americanization of both
immigrants and their newspapers, foreign-language journalism

continues to survive in the United States. Its numbers are less than one-quarter of what they were during the pre-World War I heyday, but in 1980 29 dailies printed in 13 different languages were still being published in America. Perhaps 300 weeklies, magazines, and journals in languages from Arabic to Yiddish were read by millions of first-, second- and even third-generation immigrants. And changing immigration patterns meant the birth of new foreign-language publications. In the mid-1970s when thousands of Vietnamese refugees came to America, a dynamic and varied Vietnamese press emerged.

"Our great cities," wrote Robert Park in 1922, "are mosaics of little language colonies, cultural enclaves, each maintaining its separate communal existence within the wider circle of the city's cosmopolitan life." Each enclave, he noted, supports its own press. Although the nationalities of some of the immigrant groups have changed, urban centers of the 1980s are no different than they were in Park's day. As long as there are people with common racial, national, or cultural interests, as long as there is pride in ethnicity, there will be a foreign-language press.

REFERENCES

The following material aided in the preparation of this chapter and is suggested for further reading:

Brown, Francis J. and Roucek, Joseph S. *One America.* Englewood Cliffs, NJ: Prentice-Hall, 1960.
Gutierrez, Felix F., ed. "A Spanish-Language Media Issue." *Journalism History*, IV (Summer 1977).
Handlin, Oscar. *The Uprooted.* New York: Grosset & Dunlap, 1951.
Hansen, Marcus Lee. *The Immigrant in American History.* Cambridge, MA: *Harvard University Press,* 1940.
Higham, John. *Strangers in the Land: Patterns of American Nativism 1860-1925,* 2nd ed. New York: Atheneum, 1978.
Howe, Irving. *World of Our Fathers.* New York: Harcourt Brace Jovanovich, 1976.
Hunter, Edward. *In Many Voices.* Norman Park, GA: Norman College, 1960.
Kowalik, Jan. *The Polish Press in America.* San Francisco: R & E Research Associates, 1978.
Marzolf, Marion T. *The Danish Language Press in America.* New York: Arno Press, 1979.

Miller, Edmund E. *The Hundred Year History of the German Correspondent, Baltimore, Maryland*. Baltimore: Baltimore Correspondent Publishing, 1941.

Olszyk, E. G. *The Polish Press in America*. Milwaukee: Marquette University Press, 1940.

Park, Robert E. *The Immigrant Press and Its Control*. New York: Harper & Brothers, 1922.

Smith, William Carlson. *Americans in the Making*. New York: Appleton-Century, 1939.

Soltes, Mordecai. *The Yiddish Press: An Americanizing Agency*. New York: Teachers College, Columbia University, 1925.

Wittke, Carl F. *German-Americans and the World War*. Columbus: Ohio State Archaeological & Historical Society, 1935; Reprint ed. New York: J. S. Ozer, 1974.

6

WORKING-CLASS RADICALS

A radical group without a paper is a contradiction in terms.

—Max Schachtman, Trotskyist

Anarchists, socialists, communists, populists, Marxists, syndicalists, Trotskyists, Weisbordites, Lovestoneites—the American radical left is a dizzying array of movements, parties, and splinter groups. American society was sick, they said, but exactly what the illness was or what the cure might be were matters of intense, often vitriolic, and frequently internally debilitating debate. Some saw capitalism as the ultimate evil and called for the creation of a worker-run state. Others saw the state as the ultimate evil and called for its immediate dissolution. Some worked for collectivity; others for individuality. Some wanted reform; others would settle for nothing less than revolution. But throughout the nineteenth and twentieth centuries, they all agreed on one thing: Journalism was essential to the cause.

An astonishingly large number of radical activists—including most of the nationally known organizers and leaders—devoted much of their energies to producing newspapers and journals for their movements. In fact, writes historian Joseph Conlin, "no other facet of radical political activity . . . not strikes, not subversion, not demonstrations, not terrorism, not oratory . . . claimed more attention or time." American radicals deemed the publication of some sort of periodical so vital to the cause that even splinter groups numbering no more than a few dozen members issued newspapers and theoretical journals. Although most radical publications were short-lived, and few of the groups enjoyed more than a brief heyday, various brands of radicalism captured the imagination of millions of Americans during the nineteenth and twentieth centuries.

Beginning in the early 1800s, gathering force in the decades after the Civil War and culminating in the early twentieth century, anarchism attracted both immigrant and American-born followers. Any form of government, said the anarchists, was oppressive and should be abolished. Anarchists made headlines in 1886 when several were accused of instigating the bloody Haymarket Riots in Chicago, in 1892 when Polish-born anarchist Alexander Berkman attempted to assassinate the head of Carnegie Steel Company, and in 1901 when a man calling himself an anarchist killed President William McKinley. But thousands of Americans who never used violent methods were part of the anarchist movement, including hundreds of men and women who turned to oratory and journalism to spread their philosophy. The United States was home to more than 100 anarchist publications.

During the final three decades of the nineteenth century hundreds of thousands of farmers in the South, Midwest, and West participated in the Populist movement. Calling for marketing and purchasing cooperatives, government subsidies and elastic "greenback" currency, farmers joined county, state, and regional alliances that became the backbone of a powerful nationwide third-party movement. They were led by stump lecturers and hundreds of their own reform newspapers. The editors formed a national reform press association to coordinate propaganda and education efforts that, by the mid-1890s, numbered more than 1,000 members. In that decade, the culmination of the Populist movement, more than 900 newspapers and periodicals were devoted solely to this radical farmers' movement.

The Socialist Party, organized in the 1870s by German immigrants and Americanized in the 1890s, grew to prominence in the early twentieth century. In 1900 the party had less than 10,000 members and was represented by perhaps 30 socialist newspapers, periodicals, and journals. By 1912, with party members numbering more than 100,000 and socialists serving in hundreds of elected positions, more than 300 avowedly socialist periodicals were being published in the United States. During the party's pre-World War I heyday, at least 600 different socialist periodicals were published.

Splitting from the already warring socialist movement shortly after the Soviet Revolution of 1917, American communists believed that a worker revolt, not electoral politics, was the way to achieve victory. Throughout the 1920s and 1930s the communists split into a number of factions that reflected the divisiveness of the Russian experience. Each faction issued its own publications. Internal party organs, theoretical journals, youth newspapers, weekly propaganda sheets, and one long-lived daily were all part of the communist press.

FUNCTIONS OF THE RADICAL PRESS

Although messages in the radical press differed substantially according to the beliefs of individual groups and parties, the goals were similar. Radicals felt they had discovered the cure for societal ills, and their publications were designed to spread the word. Had it been possible for radicals to use the conventional, mass circulation journals of their time for this purpose, many undoubtedly would have opted for this efficient way of reaching millions of Americans. But their ideas were inimical to the society in which they lived. Mainstream publications, seeing it as their responsibility to speak to and for the homogeneous middle, closed their pages to radical ideas, although they could hardly avoid covering events like strikes and demonstrations. Additionally, the conventional media were capitalist businesses and, like other American businesses, must have felt threatened by radical ideas concerning cooperative ownership and sharing of the wealth. Denied access the the mainstream media, radicals started their own periodicals to create a forum for their ideas and a counterbalance to the antiradical sentiment in the conventional press.

Capitalist newspapers, wrote a communist journalist in 1919, "were flooded with a deluge of falsehoods that turned them into fathomless morasses of mendacity in which truth could only be hit by accident." Wrote a socialist ten years later: "It is the rule of the capitalist papers to knife the labor movement whenever there is a chance to do so. . . . This is why we have to have a press of our own." Radicals used their myriad publications to explain their philosophies, goals, and ideas, hoping to strengthen the will of their comrades and convert those outside the movement. Writing about the working and living conditions of the urban poor, government corruption and corporate insensitivity, they criticized the American political, economic, and social systems. Their papers were used as organizational tools, publicizing events and meetings and supporting radical candidates for office.

Many publications surveyed the radical environment both in America and abroad. Labor organization, strikes, marches, demonstrations, and speeches were covered in full. News of the international workers' movement filled the pages of communist journals, and especially during the Russian Revolution and both world wars, radical publications devoted much space to international news.

But radical journals also served internal purposes. While some publications were aimed at the unconverted, others provided a means of intraparty communication. Here radicals argued ideology, clarified their goals, set up the internal structure of their organizations, and bolstered morale. Groups united by ideology but separated by geography shared progress reports. But some intraparty papers had another purpose: dissension. Factions, splitting from main groups, used their internal publications to criticize the policies of the main group and disparage other splinter groups. Carrying on a war of words, they jockeyed for position within the radical movement.

Whether they saw their purpose as external or internal communication, radical journals of all stripes shared at least one problem: money. Anticapitalist publications naturally contained no consumer advertising. In those publications that accepted advertising—many did not—commercial messages were usually limited to announcements of radical books, pamphets, and journals. Without financial support from advertising, radical journals had to depend on subscription and single-copy revenue and money alloted from the coffers of their parties. But here they were in trouble again. Many potential readers were laborers who could barely afford to buy food, let alone newspapers. For this reason, too, the parties or factions were poorly funded, and their finances were constantly being drained by lecture tours, organizational expenses, and support for striking workers. Radical publications were almost always run at a loss, and their editors and writers received little pay if any. These men and women devoted much of their lives to journalism because they believed, as the masthead of one radical newspaper proclaimed: "The power to transmit ideas is the power to change the world."

THE AGRARIAN REVOLT

The idea that "plain people" could gain control of their own lives and futures was at the heart of the agrarian populist revolt. Although Populists were, in a sense, conservatives who sought to rescue the dying tradition of agrarian self-sufficiency, their program was radical. They called for the establishment of farmer-owned marketing and purchasing cooperatives, limitations on land ownership, government ownership of railroads, telephones, and telegraphs, and an extensive overhaul of the American monetary system. Their grassroots movement emerged from farmers' experiences in the decade following the Civil War.

With money in short supply (the government's cure for inflation was to hold the supply of money at existing levels while both the population and the economy expanded), southern farmers were forced into a crop lien system that kept them impoverished and at the mercy of merchants. In order to pay off winter debts, farmers gave merchants the title to their next year's crops, thus establishing a cycle of indebtedness that was difficult to break. To escape, farmers moved to Texas where they found, in addition to mercenary merchants and rate-gouging railroad men, inadequate rainfall and hardscrabble land. It was in Texas in 1877, in response to these conditions, that the Farmers Alliance was formed. At first an apolitical self-help organization, the alliance helped farmers form marketing and purchasing cooperatives. But the opposition stimulated by the cooperative movement—from merchants, buyers, wholesale houses, bankers, and railroad—gave farmers new insights into their relationship with the commercial elements of American society and served to radicalize and politicize the movement.

Functions of the Populist Press

State and regional alliances set up networks of traveling lecturers who, from the 1870s through the mid-1890s, attempted to spread populist doctrine to farmers throughout the South and Midwest. But this was a cumbersome and time-consuming way to educate, organize, and propagandize. Alliances organized mass meetings, rallies, and conventions hoping to make their propaganda efforts both more dramatic and more efficient. But farmers were scattered over vast stretches of land, and few had the time to travel by buggy to far-away gatherings. The best way to reach them was through the press. Looking at the conventional press of their day, Populists saw that newspapers either failed to give coverage to farm reform meetings and speeches or ridiculed populist ideas. Because the mainstream press was itself a for-profit industry and depended on other for-profit businesses for advertising, Populists felt the press had a stake in defending the current economic system. The cooperative movement and greenback economics did not and could not get a fair shake in the conventional press, they said. What they needed was a press of their own.

The populist press, established in almost every state in the South, Midwest, and West, performed the complementary functions of educating farmers and attacking exploiters, monopolists, and corporations. To embrace Populism, farmers needed to understand the economic and political ramifications of the rapid growth of industry, banking, and railroads. They needed to see how their own economic fate was tied to America's financial policies. Wrote a Populist editor and author of an alliance handbook for Kansas farmers: "A thoroughly informed people cannot be enslaved, nor kept in slavery long after they become educated concerning the means used to bind them." The reformers had abiding faith in education as the farmers' salvation. A political cartoon in the Populist *American Non-Conformist* showed a working man lashed to the stake by ropes labeled "mortgages, cornered markets, railroad monopoly, telegraph monopoly." A female figure clad in flowing robes was about to cut the ropes with a sword labeled "Education." In issue after issue reform journals offered well-reasoned and sober articles on the American economic and political systems and populist plans and solutions.

Editors explained to their readers how to set up marketing and purchasing cooperatives that would allow farmers to control a larger part of their operation. Stressing the financial impact of railroad monopolies—farmers had to get their goods to market and monopoly-owned railroads could, and sometimes did, charge exorbitant rates—populist newspapers called for public (government) ownership of all the means of transportation and communication. Repeatedly and painstakingly, editors discussed the Populists' plan for monetary reform, which called for the government to issue paper money (greenbacks) as a medium of exchange and not as a commodity with intrinsic (gold-backed) value. Tight money, the editors reminded their readers, was what forced farmers to mortgage their land and their future crops just to keep operating. Editors also educated their readers about the Populists' subtreasury plan, a system combining government-owned warehouses, where farmers could store their crops, with low-interest government loans for produce placed in storage.

But alongside the calm, educational articles were fiery attacks on the evils of modern society and those whom the Populists believed were responsible for the powerless and destitute condition of farmers. When the means of production and distribution are run by monopolies, wrote the editor of *The Advocate,* "the few are benefited and the many are deprived of fair opportunities in life." The editor of the Lincoln, Nebraska *Wealth Makers* put it more forcefully: "Why must men labor without gain in order that others gain without labor? It is robbery; it is slavery." With angry rhetoric and pointed political cartoons, populist newspapers lambasted railroad owners, industry monopolists, bankers, politicians, and land specu-lators.

Editors made little distinction between news and editorial comment. Although they covered meetings, speeches, and election campaigns, their main purpose was to educate and propagandize for the cause. Most articles in the Populist press looked more like today's editorials than news stories, for editors freely expressed their personal opinions even when writing about news events. When offering their readers stories about railroad owners or bankers, editors did not present balanced coverage. They attacked.

Scope of the Populist Press

No other radical or reform group in America was as journalis-tically active as the Populists. Several thousand different populist journals were published during the life of the move-ment, ranging from the 100,000-circulation *National Economist* to countless rural weeklies that reached only a few hundred subscribers. During the 1890s alone Populists published more than 1,000 journals. In Kansas and Texas, where the Farmers

Alliance was the strongest, Populists published close to 300 newspapers and periodicals. Most journals were the organs of county, state, and regional alliances, but some were the efforts of unaffiliated Populists.

One of the best known of the unaffiliated newspapers was Henry Vincent's *American Nonconformist*. Vincent was 24 when he started publishing his journal in 1886. Although the alliance movement had not yet gained prominence in Kansas, home of the *Nonconformist*, when Vincent started publishing, he set up exchanges with other agrarian and labor newspapers. "This journal," wrote Vincent in the inaugural issue, "will aim to publish such matters as will tend to the education of the laboring classes, the farmers and the producer.... Promising to take the side of the oppressed as against the oppressor," Vincent kept a nationwide watch on political and economic activities on behalf of the underdog. The *Nonconformist* died in 1891, probably due to financial problems.

Tom Watson, a leader of agrarian malcontents in Georgia who served in the House as a Populist and later became the Populist nominee for vice president (1896) and president (1904), started his own newspaper in 1891 because one of his political enemies was editor of the state's official Alliance journal. Watson's *People's Party Paper*, issued weekly for eight years, declared its intention to "educate our people upon governmental questions, to assail official corruption, to oppose class-rule [and] legislative favoritism." It also devoted a significant amount of space to celebrating the virtues and accomplishments of Tom Watson. Although the paper sometimes had a press run of 20,000, it rarely had more than 500 paid subscribers. Money was always a problem for papers not affiliated with an alliance group.

Alliance-backed papers, which increased circulation as the organization gathered new members, could sometimes depend on the group for finances. In North Carolina, Leonidas Polk's Alliance-backed *Progressive Farmer* increased its circulation from 1,200 to 12,000 as the state organization gained prominence. Like many Populist journalists, Polk was also a party leader, elected vice president of the National Alliance in 1887 and president in 1889. Charles Macune, Alliance president in 1887, was also editor of the Alliance's national newspaper, the *National Economist*. Underwritten by the powerful Texas Alliance, the paper was considered the best edited journal of agricultural economics in the country. Its circulation surpassed 100,000.

When the agrarian movement spread through Kansas in 1889—more than 75,000 Kansans joined the Alliance in nine months—newspapers were not far behind. *The Advocate*, the official journal, reached a peak circulation of 80,000 and dozens of other Populist weeklies sprang up throughout the state. At the same time, the Alliance was spreading through the Dakotas. Farmers formed cooperative exchanges, developed an internal lecturing network, and established their own organizational newspaper, *The Ruralist*. The Minnesota Alliance attracted 15,000 members and began publishing *The Great West*, its offical newspaper. In Alabama, an Alliance stronghold, at least 100 agrarian reform newspapers were published in the 1890s, including the official *Alliance Herald*, one of the state's most widely circulated journals. As the Alliance spread westward, farmers in Bozeman, Butte, and Missoula, Montana all started their own Populist newspapers, and agrarian reformers in Oregon established the *Portland Farmers Journal* and later the *People's Party Post* to support the movement.

The National Reform Press Association

Established at the National Alliance's 1891 convention, the National Reform Press Association eventually united more than 1,000 Populist newspapers nationwide and became the propaganda arm of the People's Party. Despite various political differences, reform editors supported both the association and each other, meeting regularly, helping one another financially, and praising (in print) each other's newspapers. United both by their problems—financial woes and harassment from political and journalistic enemies—and their driving moral purpose, the editors established an internal communications network. The association provided its members with a weekly two-page ready-to-print insert with the latest party news, which became the interior of many small Populist weeklies across the nation.

Most of the editors, stressing education rather than office-seeking, remained true to the Populist doctrine of greenback economics even after the party itself adopted a "free silver" plank and nominated William Jennings Bryan (a free silver, not a greenback advocate) as its 1896 presidential candidate. Only a handful of editors supported the party's new economic doctrine of silver-backed currency; most editors dropped out of both the party and the press association. When the association held a national meeting the year after Bryan's defeat, only seven editors answered the call. But during the few years it existed, the National Reform Press Association was, in the words of historian Lawrence Goodwin, "the foremost internal achievement of the People's Party."

Effects of the Populist Press

Without the Populist press, it is doubtful whether farmers or others would have been exposed to the wide range of agrarian reform ideas. The conventional press rarely discussed the economic issues raised by Populists, either ridiculing them out of hand or reverting to sectionalist rhetoric. (Populism was denigrated or dismissed by northern and midwestern papers because its origins were in the deep South.) The New York *Times* called the subtreasury plan one of the wildest . . . projects ever seriously considered by sober man," giving the plan no serious discussion. The Alliance, said the New York *Sun*, was a bunch of "hayseed socialists" and their ideas were "specimens of absurdities." A Kansas newspaper called the movement "nauseating" and described one Populist leader as "a shyster, a fraud and an anarchist." A Nebraska daily suggested southern Populists would attempt to resurrect the Confederacy. Farmers had to turn to the Populist press to learn about movement ideas. As powerful educational and propaganda organs, populist newspapers were instrumental in converting farmers to the cause.

The Populist crusade, as carried forth in the pages of thousands of reform journals, bore fruit in the form of many legislative measures. America abandoned the gold standard and Congress enacted a variety of agricultural reforms that created, in essence, the subtreasury plan the Populists had fought for. Government subsidies to farmers, once described as an "imbecilic plan," were granted. The general electoral reform the Populists called for—woman suffrage, direct election of senators, initiative, referendum and recall—were later adopted. Populist editors, wrote one student of the movement, "were not voices crying in the wilderness, but were . . . the printed expression of the demands of a large segment of the American population." Through the reform press, those demands were heard.

THE ANARCHIST PRESS

While Populists believed in democratic reform and called for the government to play a larger role in the economic life of the nation, anarchists felt all government, regardless of form, was oppressive. The state, said anarchists, perpetuates class rule, represses the full development of the individual, and is, by its very nature, coercive. Although all anarchists believed the state must be abolished before people could freely seek their own means of self-fulfillment, they differed on how this should be accomplished. Some thought propaganda, through oratory and journalism, would convert the nation to their philosophy. Others felt direct revolutionary action—"propaganda by deed"—was needed. The movement was an example of both "home-grown" radicalism (many of its leaders were native-born Americans reacting to conditions in American society) and foreign-inspired radicalism (German immigrants were major contributors to the movement). Within the anarchist movement subgroups flourished. Anarcho-communists and collectivist anarchists stressed class consciousness and called for organized action by workers. Anarcho-syndicalists backed radical labor. Anarcho-pacifists devoted their energies to antiwar efforts. Sometimes the overlap among the anarchist, socialist, and communist movements was so extensive that Party distinctions blurred entirely.

Emergence of the Anarchist Press

Josiah Warren, a New England-born social reformer who is regarded as the founder of philosophical anarchism in America, began his radical activities in the late 1820s. Although he had been a member of the Owenite utopian community at New Harmony, he soon turned from collectivism to extreme individualism. After developing the theory that the price of a commodity ought to be based solely on the cost of producing it, he established the Time Store in Cincinnati to put his ideas into practice. Here customers bartered their labor or the goods they produced for items in the store. When pressure from local advertisers caused the Cincinnati press to ignore his experiment, Warren decided to publish his own newspaper. In January of 1833 he issued *The Peaceful Revolutionist,* the first anarchist newspaper in America. The four-page weekly, which expanded on Warren's labor equity principle and proclaimed the absolute sovereignity of the individual, died four months later because of lack of subscribers. But Warren's influence continued. Later he founded an anarchist community on Long Island, New York which lasted for 12 years, published a full-length treatise on the philosophy of anarchism, and proselytized for the cause.

One of the people Warren converted was Benjamin Tucker, a man who believed journalism was the key to converting America to anarchism. Tucker edited *The Word,* an anarchist publication, in 1877 and in the same year started his periodical, *The Radical Review.* Unable to secure enough subscribers to keep *The Review* afloat, Tucker ceased publication ten months later and took positions first at the Boston *Globe* and then at *Engineering* magazine to finance his career in radical journalism. From 1881 to 1908 he published *Liberty,* a fortnightly advocating the sovereignty of the individual and laissez-faire capitalism. The journal, reaching fewer than 1,000 subscribers, carried reprints of anarchist essays, translations of European anarchist literature, letters to the editor, and strongly worded editorials. While he was publishing *Liberty,* Tucker also started his own publishing company, which issued translations of French and Russian anarchist books as well as several American and British anarchist treatises.

Propaganda versus Propaganda by Deed

While Tucker was advocating individual anarchism achieved through peaceful means, another group of anarchists was calling for the violent overthrow of the state. Johann Most, an exiled German revolutionary, edited the German-language *Freiheit,* which carried articles on manufacturing bombs and nitroglycerine explosives. Albert Parsons, an Alabama-born ex-socialist, edited *Alarm,* an anarchist journal that railed against the injustices suffered by workers and included articles on incendiary devices. *Truth,* a third "propaganda by deed" publication, carried the motto: "Truth is five cents a copy and dynamite is forty cents a pound."

In the 1880s a group of radicals combined Most's anarchist ideas with an interest in trade union organization to become proponents of anarcho-syndicalism. In Chicago they found fertile ground. There, during the first few months 1886, strikers, strike breakers, and police had clashed repeatedly at the McCormick Harvester Company plant. On May 6, August Spies, editor of the German-language anarchist *Die Arbeiter Zeitung,* spoke to a labor meeting. After leaving the meeting, some strikers clashed with strike breakers, and one person was killed and several wounded. The Chicago press mistakenly reported that six had died and placed full blame on the strikers. The next day Spies, Albert Parsons, and several other anarchist leaders held a protest meeting in Chicago's Haymarket Square. During one of the surprisingly peaceful speeches, a bomb was thrown from near the platform, killing 11 people and wounding several hundred. The bomb thrower was never identified, but Spies, Parsons, and six other anarchist leaders were indicted based on the incendiary statements they had made in the anarchist press. Spies, Parsons, and two other anarchists were found guilty of inciting to murder and were hanged. Another convicted anarchist committed suicide in prison. In 1893, Illinois governor Peter Altgeld pardoned the remaining anarchists, calling the trial a travesty of justice.

"Propaganda by deed" anarchism suffered irreparable damage because of the Haymarket Riot, the trial, and the torrent of negative publicity. Although Leon Czolgosz, a man who claimed to be an anarchist but who belonged to no anarchist organization, assassinated President William McKinley in 1901, this brand of anarchism found few followers and fewer journalistic proponents after 1886.

Government Suppression

Although anarchists were no longer advocating the violent overthrow of the government, their philosophy was still threatening to the American system. In 1902, New York State passed a law prohibiting the publication and distribution of anarchist literature. In 1903, Congress enacted immigration legislation banning alien anarchists from entering the United States. In 1917 and 1918 the Espionage and Sedition Acts made the publication of disloyal or un-American statements punishable by up to ten years' imprisonment. But still anarchists continued speaking and writing.

Probably the most famous anarchist publication of the time was Emma Goldman's *Mother Earth*. Goldman, a Russian-born radical who came to the United States in 1886, used her monthly journal to propagandize for anarchism, labor unionism, feminism, and civil liberties. *Mother Earth* was also an important medium for the arts, publishing the writing of Tolstoi, Dostoevsky, Thoreau, and Whitman. In 1917, invoking a provision of the Espionage Act, postal authorities banned *Mother Earth* from the mails because it advocated nonintervention in World War I and opposed the draft. Goldman immediately changed the name of the journal to *Mother Earth Bulletin* and continued publishing. But seven months later, it too was declared unmailable. At the same time, Goldman and Alexander Berkman, her co-editor, were arrested for their leadership of the antidraft movement and were sentenced to two years in prison. Both were deported after their release in 1919.

Despite the legal and extralegal repression of radical speakers and journalists following the Russian Revolution—the so-called Red Scare—anarchists kept publishing. *The Freeman* (1920-1923) advocated individual sovereignty and the single tax principles of Henry George. *Road to Freedom* (1924-1932) attempted to keep alive the spirit of anarchism after the movement had fallen on hard times. The product of a utopian anarchist community in New Jersey, the publication reprinted the writings of great European anarchists, presented biographical sketches of past leaders, and published articles by the exiled Goldman and Berkman. It contained little current news about the American anarchist movement, for the movement was dormant.

Anarchist Press 1930-1950

Various radical philosophies including anarchism gained new adherents in the 1930s. *Vanguard* (1932-1939) attempted to Americanize European anarchist doctrines, calling for a society based on industrial unions and decentralized communes. Criticizing foreign-language anarchist publications for limiting their scope to immigrant groups, *Vanguard* tried to appeal to American-born laborers and intellectuals. In San Francisco,

Man! (1933-1940) offered West Coast radicals lengthy theoretical discussions of anarchist philosophy.

But the longest lived, most successful anarchist paper of the time was *The Catholic Worker.* Founded in 1933 by Dorothy Day, a Greenwich Village leftist who dramatically converted to Catholicism in the 1920s, the paper combined Catholic piety with anarcho-pacifism. "The fundamental aim of most radical sheets is conversion of its readers to radicalism and atheism," wrote Day in the first issue. "Is it not possible to be radical and not atheist?" Day's monthly took up the causes of civil liberties, workers' rights, and nonviolence and through the years helped to radicalize small but visible groups of Catholic clergy and laity. *The Catholic Worker* reached more than 150,000 readers in the 1930s. Although its circulation was less than a third of that in the 1950s, 20 years later when the pacifism it preached gained respectability during the Vietnam war, circulation shot up to 100,000. Dorothy Day continued editing the journal until just before her death, at 83, in 1980.

In the war and postwar years, American anarchists had no movement to speak of, but they still had journals to read. *Politics* (1944-1949) flirted with a variety of leftist philosophies before settling on anarchism. *Retort* (1942-1951), one of the most sophisticated journals of anarchist literature, specialized in social philosophy and the arts. Holley Cantine, an artist, craftsman, and philosopher, wrote, edited, typeset, printed, and circulated the quarterly publication. *The Match* and *Libertarian*, both founded in 1956, expounded on individual sovereignty and civil liberties.

Effects of the Anarchist Press

The anarchist press was the backbone of the American anarchist movement. It gave the movement a theoretical base, helped attract followers, and aided internal organization and communication. Even when there was no movement to report on, anarchists kept publishing newspapers and periodicals to keep their ideas alive. Without these publications, it is doubtful whether such unpopular concepts would have any public forum in this country.

Although the anarchists' primary objective—to create a country with no laws and no government to stifle the development of its citizens—gained little favor with mainstream society, other ideas promoted by the movement and its press did find acceptance. Trade unionism and workers' rights, two basic tenets of anarcho-syndicalism, are no longer considered radical ideas. The anarchists' cause of civil liberties has been taken up by a variety of American groups, some of them quite conservative, and the Supreme Court has generally supported the cause. Pacifism, so unpopular during the two world wars, achieved respectability during the Vietnam era.

THE SOCIALIST PRESS

While agrarian movements believed all government was inherently repressive and called for its abolition, socialists wanted a powerful government run by—or at least in the interests of—the working class. Like the anarchists, they split over how to achieve their goal. Some factions called for revolutionary action; others promoted radical trade unionism; still others believed in working within the democratic reform process. Throughout the late nineteenth and early twentieth centuries, the movement was wracked by internal battles, many of which took place in the pages of factional newspapers. Like anarchism, the socialist movement took its cues from both native-born radicals and foreign-born contributors.

Socialism in the Nineteenth Century

In the 30 years following the Civil War, the United States changed from an agricultural nation to a mighty industrial power. The same process in Europe resulted in a vigorous socialist movement, yet in America the transformation was a quiet one. The trauma of the Civil War made Americans reluctant to enter into another internal conflict. And the American ideal—if not the reality—of a classless society meant that socialist ideas of class consciousness and class politics were not easily accepted.

It is not surprising, then, that the early socialist movement was limited to a portion of the immigrant population. The Socialist Labor Party (SLP), organized in 1876, was a small group of German radical intellectuals. The first socialist newspaper, *Republik der Arbeiter,* was German. Not until 1890, when an erstwhile professor of international law at Columbia University took over leadership of the SLP, did the organization expand its membership beyond the German-language community.

Daniel DeLeon, the powerful leader who changed the party to a broad-based organization that scored several electoral victories, started the SLP's first regular English-language publication. *The Weekly People* was designed to propagandize among the native-born. But the paper, like its editor, was endlessly combative. Dogmatic and doctrinaire, DeLeon always seemed to be purging someone from the party. As his mouthpiece, *The Weekly People* may have done more to fracture the movement than to unite it.

Weakened by DeLeon's authoritarian leadership, the severe economic depression of 1893, and the failure of numerous workers' strikes, the socialist movement split asunder. One group stayed with DeLeon; another faction gravitated toward moderate reformism; a third group split to become the Socialist Party of America (SPA) under the leadership of the popular labor organizer Eugene V. Debs. Each group started journals to attract new members and cast aspersions on the other factions.

The Industrial Workers of the World

Founded in Chicago in 1905, the Industrial Workers of the World (IWW) was a diverse group of radicals who had little in common other than their anger with the American Federal of Labor's monopoly of unionism and its refusal to organize unskilled workers. At first a part of the socialist coalition, the IWW expelled DeLeon, opting for radical unionism rather than the SLP's revolutionary political action. Later the SPA purged the IWW, attempting to play down class struggle in order to make electoral gains. In the first decade and a half of the twentieth century, the IWW recruited tens of thousands of unskilled workers, conducted more than 150 strikes, and published at least 70 newspapers and periodicals. "They had a compulsion to publish," wrote an historian of the movement, "and a positive knack for the craft."

Industrial Worker (1908-1918), published in Spokane and Seattle, preached labor radicalism among migratory farm workers, lumberjacks, and miners. A full-sized weekly, the paper covered regional labor conflicts and free speech battles, becoming the official organ of the IWW's western region contingent. It mixed political cartoons and book reviews with ideological treatises and theoretical commentaries. Washington, a hotbed of IWW activity, was also home to *Why?* (1913-1914), an intellectual rather than a political journal, and *The Agitator* (1910-1913, later *The Syndicalist*), an unaffiliated IWW propaganda sheet. *The Industrial Unionist* in Portland and *New Unionist* in Los Angeles also kept tabs on West Coast labor radicalism.

In Chicago, home of the IWW, *Industrial Union Bulletin* (1907-1909) propagandized for direct trade union organization and became a forum for anti-DeLeon rhetoric. *The One Big Union Monthly*, published by the IWW's executive board, functioned as a national bulletin for radical labor activity while proclaiming the IWW's independence from the socialist movement. *Industrial Pioneer*, its successor, was a 48-page monthly that mixed political cartoons, proletarian art, and "fables for the working class" with essays on industrial unionism and Marxism. Weakened by its opposition to World War I, and later by postwar prosperity, the IWW became more of a propaganda organization than a labor-organizing group. *Industrial Pioneer* reflected the change, offering its readers educational, philosophical, and historical articles. The paper died in 1926, nine years before the Congress of Industrial Organizations fulfilled the IWW's dream of unionizing unskilled workers.

The Heyday of Socialism

In 1900, a few socialists held political office and party membership was below 10,000. Twelve years later, America had a socialist congressman, 79 socialist mayors in 24 states, numerous state legislators and elected officials in more than 300 municipalities. More than 1,000 socialists held office in

1912, the year in which almost one million Americans voted for SPA leader Eugene V. Debs for president. In that same year, 323 avowedly socialist publications were being issued in the United States, including several large-circulation dailies. The socialists' faith in the power of radical journalism to recruit, convert, and organize knew no bounds. "Sure the comrades wanted a daily," remarked one Midwest organizer. "How else could we hope to capture the state without a daily newspaper?"

One of the most successful socialist dailies of the time was the *Milwaukee Leader*. In 1910, Milwaukee radicals sent a socialist to Congress, elected a socialist mayor, and captured 21 of 35 seats on the city council. Two months after the election, the city's socialists voted to transform the *Social-Democrat Herald*—a weekly that started in Chicago in 1898 and moved to Milwaukee in 1901—into the daily *Milwaukee Leader*. They felt they needed a strong daily to counter the "hateful misrepresentations of the Socialist administration" they found in Milwaukee's capitalist press. "We shall preach no class hatred," wrote editor Victor Berger in the first issue, "but we will preach class consciousness six days a week."

During its first week of publication in 1911, the *Leader* found it necessary to send out squads to protect its newsboys from being beaten or harassed. Still, its average daily circulation exceeded 31,000 during the first month of operation. When the paper was two months old, it was on sale at more than 300 newsstands across the country and was reaching readers as far away as California and Alaska. The *Leader* suffered great readership and revenue losses when Berger was indicted under the Espionage Act (because the *Leader* opposed U.S. intervention in World War I) and the post office refused to deliver its mail. It changed ownership several times in the 1920s and 1930s but continued as a liberal, labor-oriented daily until 1942.

Socialist dailies were also being published in New York and Cleveland, and California was home to the largest-circulation socialist magazine in the world, *Wilshire's Magazine*. Dubbed "The Millionaire Socialist," Gaylord Wilshire (after whom Wilshire Boulevard was named) started his magazine in 1900. Subsidized with $100,000 of his own money, the magazine attracted close to 300,000 subscribers, offering them commentary on international and national events, union and IWW news, interviews with prominent socialists, book reviews, and fiction. Other publications that flourished during the socialists' heyday included *The International Socialist Review* (1900-1918), a strong supporter of labor that reached 40,000 subscribers by 1911, and various internal party organs like *Socialist Party Monthly Bulletin* and *The Party Builder*.

But the most famous of all socialist journals during these heady times was a Greenwich Village literary and political journal called *The Masses* (1911-1917). It was, in the words of its editor Max Eastman, "a revolutionary and not a reform magazine; a magazine with no dividends to pay; a free magazine; frank, arrogant, impertinent, searching for true causes." Unaffiliated with any particular socialist faction and flirting with both socialism and anarchism, *The Masses* supported radical ideas from the workers' revolution to the sexual revolution and served as a vital forum for both art and politics. It was a visually bold, large-size magazine that presented its readers with an eclectic mix of serious theoretical treatises, satirical fiction, dramatic artwork, up-to-the-minute reports on labor conflicts, and muckraking articles on everything from prostitution to political corruption.

The Masses, wrote one of its contributors, stood for "fun, truth, realism, freedom, peace, feminism and revolution." It was, in the words of another contributor, "the recording secretary of the revolution in the making." Both earnest and impudent, the magazine attracted the top radical journalists and artists of the day. John Reed (popularized in the movie *Reds*), Walter Lippmann, Carl Sandburg, and Sherwood Anderson wrote for *The Masses*. Famous radical cartoonist Art Young contributed biting social commentary. In one of his cartoons a slum child, gazing at the night sky, makes this heartbreaking remark: "Ooh, look at the stars. They're as thick as bedbugs."

The Masses died in 1917 after postal authorities revoked its mailing privileges and the government indicted its editors under the Espionage Act for their anti-World War I stance. But for a few years, wrote historian Irving Howe, it was "the rallying center . . . for almost everything that was then alive and irreverent in American culture."

World War I and the Socialist Press

Many socialists were not pacifists. While they accepted the necessity of revolutionary violence to achieve their goals, they strenuously objected to U.S. intervention in World War I, saying that modern war benefited only capitalists. They saw the war as a struggle between imperialist powers who sent legions of their working-class citizens to die on the battlefield. Both before and after the United States joined the fray, socialist publications decried the war and frequently counseled draft resistance and evasion. For this they were punished (see Chapter 7).

Two months after the United States declared war, Congress passed the Espionage Act, a legal mechanism for suppressing antiwar sentiment and punishing those who attempted to cause insubordination, disloyalty, or refusal of military duty. During the first year of the Espionage Act, almost 80 radical publications lost their mailing privileges and an unknown number of radical journalists were jailed. By the end of 1917 almost every important official of the IWW was in prison. In 1918, the Sedition Act expanded the definition of "disloyal speech," making it possible to prosecute additional radical journalists.

The (New York) *Revolt*, (Chicago) *Alarm,* and (San Francisco) *Blast* all had their mailing privileges revoked. *American Socialist,* the official organ of the SPA, was also declared unmailable. In Milwaukee, *Leader* editor Victor Berger and four other socialists were indicted under the Espionage Act, and in New York five editors of *The Masses* were put on trial for violating the act. On September 5, 1917 justice officials raided IWW halls throughout the country, rounding up 166 IWW leaders, orators, and journalists who had been spreading antiwar propaganda. Ninety-three were convicted and sent to prison including IWW founder William "Big Bill" Haywood.

By the end of the war, the American socialist movement was in sharp decline. Some of its most powerful journals had been silenced and many of its leaders had been jailed. Otherwise "good socialists" who disagreed with the party's persistent antiwar stance deserted the SPA. Finally, the Bolshevik revolution shattered the uneasy coalition of socialists within the SPA. The right wing defended Russia but believed the Russian experiment was not applicable to a prosperous, stable America. The left wing wanted to follow the Bolshevik example.

In 1919 the SPA split into the Socialist, Communist, and Communist Labor parties and spent the next decade warring among themselves. Membership in the right-wing Socialist Party dropped to 11,000 by 1922. The party experienced a brief surge of popularity during the Depression and continued to publish a variety of journals into the mid- and late twentieth century, but it never again achieved its pre-World War I prominence.

THE COMMUNIST PARTY PRESS

The left-wing socialists who split from the SPA to form the Communist Party (CP) and the Communist Labor Party (CLP) differed sharply from the SPA on matters of tactics and leadership. The two communist parties, which merged to become the Communist Party of the United States in 1922, believed the success of socialism in America hinged on following Russia's example. Although many of its followers and some of its leaders were idealistic young Americans, the party looked to Moscow for orders, believing it could replicate the Russian peasant revolution among the American working class. Thus party policy was not an independent application of Marxist principles based on the study of U.S. conditions, but rather a set of ideas emerging from and relevant to the Soviet experience.

Throughout the 1920s the Communist Party and the SPA battled one another, vying for the affections of the working class during the 1924-1925 coal strike and the 1926 Passaic textile strike. In 1924 the rift deepened when Robert "Fighting Bob" LaFollette, the Progressive Party candidate for president, accepted SPA support but ousted the communists in his coalition. Not only did the two wings of the socialist movement war against each other, but the Communist Party warred internally. Following the example of the purge-happy Soviets, the party regularly expelled dissident members, spending its energy on ideological hairsplitting and organizational trivia.

The Press and Internal Dissent in the 1920s

Factionalism not only debilitated the political power of the socialist movement, it crippled its propaganda efforts and, of course, the chief agency of that propaganda, the journals. Like other radical groups, communists believed, as one organizer wrote, "the best means for the organization of the broad masses . . . is the press." Nonetheless, factional editors spent more time swatting at dissident comrades than attempting to construct a viable movement. Many of the journals no longer looked outward and forward, but became consumed with the petty infighting that characterized American radicalism after the Bolshevik Revolution.

John Reed, radical journalist and ex-*Masses* contributor, started the *New York Communist,* which waged a merciless battle against socialist right wingers. Socialists, wrote Reed in his short-lived journal, should "withdraw from active cooperation in reform movements and devote their energies to organizing the proletariat." Echoing this Soviet-inspired stance, *Class Struggle,* the theoretical journal of the CLP, called for revolutionary mass action. Socialism, the journal said, could not be attained through reform or electoral victories. It must come from a victory of the proletariat over the bourgeoisie. The CPL's official party organ, *The Revolutionary Age,* concerned itself almost solely with Russian and European news. *Communist International,* which published Russian, German, French, and English editions, reflected the inner struggles of the Soviet Communist Party.

The Daily Worker

In the early 1920s, the ten procommunist dailies published in the United States were all foreign-language newspapers. Believing the movement could go nowhere unless it attracted native-born members, the Soviet Communist Party offered its American counterpart $50,000 to start an English-language daily. Ironically, the American Party's foreign-language federations raised the additional $10,000 necessary to start the venture. Born in debt, *The Daily Worker* remained a financial drain on the party throughout its life. But the expense of the paper was rarely questioned, for the leadership believed a party that could not produce a daily paper in the language of its own country could have little claim to power.

From the start, control of *The Daily Worker* was recognized crucial by any factional group hoping to control the party. The editor-in-chief position became a political pawn that changed hands among warring factions with the editor chosen from top officialdom on the basis of political power rather than journalistic ability. The result was, until the mid-1930s, a dogmatic and humorless publication that paid more attention to internecine struggles than the movement itself.

During the Popular Front era of the 1930s—so called because the party attempted to broaden its base—*The Daily Worker* adopted a breezier style and omitted the weighty theoretical discussions of the past. The paper included features, reviews of books, films and radio shows, and even a sports page. It was probably the only non-Black newspaper to publish scores of the Negro Baseball League. During World War II it offered extensive coverage of the Eastern Front and the Red Army by developing an informal network of correspondents among communist GIs and exiled communists from occupied countries. Always in debt and never surpassing 35,000 circulation, the paper died in 1958.

Youth Organizations and the Press

"Youth steps forward upon the arena of class struggle and intends to stay there until the end," proclaimed *Youth Worker,* one of the Communist Party's many youth publications. Written by and for young people, the paper's goal was to counter the "bourgeois influence of education on youth."

Throughout the 1930s and 1940s, the Communist Party attempted to expand its membership by propagandizing among young people. The Young Communist League organized on college campuses, publishing a variety of journals during the two decades. *Student Review* and *Student Advocate* emphasized labor struggles and the development of proletarian art and literature. *Young Communist Review* interpreted the official party line, mirroring the attitude of *The Daily Worker, Champion of Youth,* published during the Popular Front days, attempted to create a radical coalition. *Clarity,* the official quarterly of the Young Communist League in the 1940s, explained the current political line to members and sympathizers.

Factionalism in the 1930s and 1940s

After Lenin's death in 1924, the Soviet Communist Party purged itself of various dissidents. Eliminating the opposition of Trotsky, Bukharin, and several other factional leaders, Stalin established himself as virtual party dictator. In the 1930s he purged the party again. The American Communist Party, taking its cues from Russia, followed suit. Trotskyists, Weisbordites, Marlenites, Lovenstoneites, and various other factions split from (or were purged from) the main party. All started their own journals.

Opposed to Stalinist leadership, the Trotskyists were a relatively small splinter group that nonetheless succeeded in publishing a weekly newspaper, a monthly theoretical review, a youth publication, and, from time to time, little newspapers in Yiddish, Greek, and Polish. *The Militant,* the group's major publication, devoted itself to building "a combat party of the working class in the tradition of Leninism."

Splitting from the Trotskyists, followers of Albert Weisbord (Weisbordites) founded the Communist League of Struggle and published their own journal, *Class Struggle.* The Weisbordites had so many defectors that eventually the group's membership was limited to Mr. and Mrs. Weisbord. Marlenites—composed of a few members of the Marlen family—were yet another Trotskyist splinter group.

The American Communist Party, a small group of dissidents purged from the main party in 1929, published *Road to Communism, Revolutionary Age,* and *Workers Age.* Called the Lovestoneites after their leader Jay Lovestone, the group stood to the right of the main party. The various factions used their journals to war against one another, thus deepening the rifts and further eroding the communist movement.

The "Red Decade" and Beyond

For a brief time in the 1930s, the Communist Party attracted distinguished artists, writers, and intellectuals. Adopting the Popular Front approach, the party attempted to expand its membership by including a variety of unaffiliated reformers and left wingers. While many factional publications continued to wage internal warfare, newspapers like *The Daily Worker* popularized their content and tried to broaden readership.

But the Popular Front idea, never much of a success anyway, died with the breakup of the Soviet-American alliance and the onset of the cold war. Post-World War II prosperity and McCarthyism further eroded the party's influence. Despite the continuing publication of a variety of journals, by the 1950s the Communist Party was the weakest of all radical sects. Although they never achieved their goal of a worker revolution, the communists—through their organizations and their publications—did create a forum for radical ideas. Some of these ideas, including unionism and workers' rights, are now a part of the American mainstream.

REFERENCES

The following material aided in the preparation of this chapter and is suggested for further reading:

Beck, Elmer, "Autopsy of a Labor Daily: The Milwaukee Leader." *Journalism Monographs,* 16 (August 1970).

Buchstein, Frederick. "The Anarchist Press in American Journalism." *Journalism History,* (Summer 1974), pp. 43-5.

Conlin, Joseph R., ed. *The American Radical Press, 1880-1960,* Vols. I and II. Westport, CT: Greenwood Press, 1974.

Destler, Chester. "Western Radicalism, 1865-1901." *Mississippi Valley Historical Review,* XXXV (December 1944), pp. 335-368.

Fried, Albert, ed. *Socialism in America.* Garden City, NY: Doubleday, 1970.

Goldwater, Walter. *Radical Periodicals in America, 1890-1950: A Bibliography with Brief Notes.* New Haven, CT: Yale University Press, 1966.

Goodwin, Lawrence. *Democratic Promise: The Populist Movement in America.* New York: Oxford University Press, 1976.

Hicks, John D. *The Populist Revolt.* Minneapolis: University of Minnesota Press, 1931.

Hofstadter, Richard. *The Age of Reform.* New York: Vintage Books, 1955.

Lutzsky, Seymour. *The Reform Editors and Their Press.* Ph.D. dissertation, State University of Iowa, 1951.

O'Neill, William L., ed. *Echoes of Revolt: The Masses 1911-1917.* Chicago: Quadrangle, 1966.

Pollack, Norman, ed. *The Populist Mind.* Indianapolis: Bobbs-Merrill, 1967.

Rocker, Rudolf. *Pioneers of American Freedom: Origin of Liberal and Radical Thought in America.* Los Angeles: Rocker Publications Committee, 1949.

Rogers, William Warren. *The One-Gallused Rebellion.* Baton Rouge: Louisiana State University Press, 1970.

Woodward, C. Vann. *Tom Watson: Agrarian Rebel.* New York: Macmillan, 1938.

7

WAR RESISTERS

> Once lead this people into war and they'll forget there ever was such a thing as tolerance. To fight you must be brutal and ruthless and the spirit of ruthless brutality will enter into every fiber of our national life.
>
> —Woodrow Wilson, 1917

When Civil War general William Tecumseh Sherman told Michigan Military Academy's graduating class "war is hell," he was referring to carnage on the battlefield. But war was no less hellish for those who refused to serve on the battlefield. For some, pacifism was the only cause; for others, an antiwar stance was part of a larger critique of American society. Impelled by personal, philosophical, religious, or political beliefs, war resisters suffered ostracism, harassment, physical abuse, and imprisonment. For many, the worst punishment of all was the denial of their First Amendment rights.

Perhaps at no other time during the life of a nation is free speech as endangered as it is during wartime. Political leaders, wanting unanimity of purpose and action, use their power to squelch dissent. The courts, noting the "clear and present danger" of dissent during wartime, uphold repressive legislation. The conventional press, supporting governmental policies and reflecting the usually dominant prowar mood of the country, not only closes its pages to dissenting ideas but frequently attacks those who go against the grain.

For those who believe war is wrong and want to propagandize against it, the choices are few. Denied access to the mainstream press, they must depend on publications of their own making. Denied First Amendment rights, they frequently suffer both persecution and prosecution.

THE GREAT WAR

It was "the war to end all wars," the war that would "make the world safe for democracy." It was also the war that led to hysterical excesses in the abridgment of civil liberties by what one historian called a "propaganda demented people." A variety of groups within the United States, together representing millions of people, voiced objections to the war both before and after America's involvement. Isolationists wanted no part of Europe's problems. Religious pacifists denounced all wars. Blacks believed it was hypocritical to fight for democracy abroad when they did not enjoy democracy at home. German and Austrian immigrants suffered from divided loyalties, and some could not support their new homeland in a war against their old homeland. Socialists of all stripes believed the war was an imperialist adventure that would benefit only capitalists. All of these war resisters used their own newspapers and periodicals to criticize U.S. policy while bolstering internal unity.

Blacks and the Fight Against Discrimination

The Black press (see Chapter 2) greeted U.S. involvement in World War I less than enthusiastically. For them, America was a land of unequal opportunity, widespread discrimination, and domestic violence. Why, they wondered, should they fight for democracy abroad when there was no democracy at home? When a Black weekly in Virginia published such a statement in 1917, the government invoked the Espionage Act and declared the paper unmailable.

Although some Black leaders and journalists steadfastly refused to support the war, the majority believed an antiwar stance would harm the Black cause in America. They supported the war but continued to criticize U.S. domestic and military policies that defined Blacks as second-class citizens. The Chicago *Defender*, probably the most militant Black paper of the time, relentlessly attacked the discrimination and segregation of Black troops. Editors of influential Black papers in New York, Boston, Baltimore, and Cleveland joined the *Defender* in exposing injustices within the military.

These attacks—even though they were published within the context of support for the war—were considered disloyal and unpatriotic. The Committee on Public Information, a war propaganda agency, insisted that the Black movement was infested with German agents who were spreading lies about the treatment of Blacks within the military. Some Black editors were threatened with imprisonment and their papers threatened with denial of mailing privileges. Although the Black press as a whole was not antiwar—in fact, several major journals fought hard for Black officers' training facilities—it was, like the antiwar press, treated as a threat to national unity.

Immigrants and Divided Loyalties

"Every man ought to love his country," said Theodore Roosevelt in 1918. "[But] he is only entitled to one country. If he claims loyalty to two countries, he is necessarily a traitor to at least one." For Roosevelt, who could trace his American lineage back to the Revolutionary War, it may have been that simple. But for millions of immigrants, loyalty to America meant severing emotional and cultural attachments to their ancestral homeland. Caught between their new loyalty to the United States and their old loyalty to Europe, immigrants—most particularly the ten million people who listed Germany as their country of origin—found themselves in a precarious position that worsened as the U.S. commitment to the Allies grew.

Not surprisingly, the German-language press (see Chapter 5) had been elated by German victories early in the war. Most expounded on the German point of view and called for U.S. neutrality. A few openly supported the Fatherland. But after America entered the war, a number of influential German-language newspapers called for support of U.S. policies. Wrote the editor of one of the largest German dailies, *Der Deutsche Correspondent:* "Keep in mind that while Germany is the land of our fathers, this is the land of our children." Some editors who could not bring themselves to declare war on their homeland stopped writing about the war entirely. Others turned to preaching pacifism. A handful continued to denounce U.S. policy.

Although the majority of German-language newspapers did support the United States, the anti-German hysteria that swept the country from 1917 to 1918 was indiscriminate. Everything German, from sauerkraut (renamed "liberty cabbage") to newspapers, was suspect. Said Teddy Roosevelt in 1917, "We are convinced that today our most dangerous foe is the foreign language press." Indeed the U.S. government was so fearful of what German-language publications (and other foreign-language papers) were telling their readers that it passed the Trading with the Enemies Act in October 1917 requiring editors to file translations of all government and war-related stories.

Those few German and Austro-Hungarian publications that continued to oppose U.S. policy after America's entry into the war did so for a variety of reasons, including (but by no means limited to) agreement with the aims of the Central Powers. For many immigrants and first-generation Americans, war meant American troops battling their relatives and friends, fighting in the trenches near the villages their families had called home for generations. Others had fled their homelands years ago seeking peace and freedom in America. For them, wrote settlement worker and peace advocate Jane Addams, "conscription and war were something which belonged to the unhappy Europe they left behind." When America declared war, "it was as if their last throw had been lost." Still others came to America with radical political ideas. As socialists they opposed the war on other grounds.

Socialists and the Capitalist War

"It is not a war for democracy," wrote Max Eastman in the June 1917 *Masses*. "It did not originate in a dispute about democracy, and it is unlikely to terminate in a democratic settlement." This was, in essence, the socialist view of World War I. When the Socialist Party met the day after the United States declared war, it proclaimed its "unalterable opposition" to the war, adding that modern wars "have always been made by the classes and fought by the masses."

The socialist press (see Chapter 6), with few exceptions, devoted itself to condemning conscription, counseling draft evasion, attacking U.S. motives for joining the war, and supporting international workers' movements. The major socialist publications of the time—*The Masses, Appeal to Reason*, and the *Milwaukee Leader*—kept up a steady stream of invective until they were silenced by the government. The official party organ, *American Socialist*, as well as scores of socialist and radical weeklies across America, joined the fight against a war they believed was a "crime against the people of the United States and the nations of the world." Regardless of which side was victorious, the workers would lose and the capitalists (particularly the munitions investors) would win, said socialist writers in editorial after editorial.

Joining the socialist publications in their fight against the war were the various International Workers of the World (IWW) newspapers and publications emerging from the Populist-socialist Nonpartisan League. Wrote one League editor: "It is a rich man's war...to protect the moneyed interests." Even some religious pacifists, notably the life-long Christian pacifist leader A. J. Muste, used class consciousness arguments to attack the immorality of the war.

Suppression, Hysteria, and the War Resisters

Suppressing antiwar journalism and harassing war resisters became a national pastime in 1917 and 1918. A number of official, semiofficial, and private organizations saw it as their patriotic duty to spy on, threaten, intimidate—and sometimes physically attack—war resisters. Organizations like the American Defense League, the American Protective League, the Sedition Slammers and the Terrible Threateners formed vigilante patrols that roamed the streets looking for antiwar speakers and pamphleteers. The New York *Times* and *Literary Digest* urged their readers to report "any utterances or writings that appeared seditious." The president of Columbia University fired professors who did not support the war. Germans, regardless of their attitude about the war, were immediately suspect.

The government quickly moved into a leadership role in the fight against war resisters, mandating that all foreign-language publications submit translations of war-related articles and establishing the Committee on Public Information as a censorship and propaganda agency. In addition to blanketing the conventional media with "official" war news, the committee also sponsored 75,000 speakers who delivered speeches in 5,000 American cities and towns arousing the "righteous wrath of the people" against Germany (and, by implication, against those who were against the war).

But the most striking attack on civil liberties during the war was the passage and enforcement of the 1917 Espionage Act and the 1918 Sedition Act. The Espionage Act gave the government the right to imprison and fine (20 years and $10,000) those found guilty of attempting to cause insubordination, disloyalty, or refusal of military service. A special section of the bill gave the Postmaster General the right to declare unmailable any material violating the act. During the six months after the act was passed, more than 1,000 men and women were prosecuted and 130 were imprisoned. The Sedition Act made it possible to prosecute additional radicals and war resisters by making it a crime to excite discontent against the government or disturb tranquility through inflammatory language.

By the fall of 1918, almost 80 newspapers and periodicals had been suppressed for anti-war articles, including most of the major socialist and IWW publications and a variety of foreign-language papers. The Department of Justice raided IWW halls in more than 30 cities, confiscating pamphlets and newspapers and arresting leaders. In three mass trials in Chicago, Sacramento, and Kansas City, 168 IWW members were convicted for their antiwar speeches and writings. During the war years perhaps as many as 10,000 American war resisters were victims of legal and extralegal suppression. Wrote Supreme Court Justice Oliver Wendell Holmes when he voted to uphold the government's right to raid a socialist bookstore and office: "When a nation is at war many things that may be said in peace are of such a hindrance to its efforts that their utterance will not be endured."

WORLD WAR II

If ever there was a war worth fighting, thought many Americans, World War II was it. Since the 1930s the United States had watched Mussolini and Hitler gain power and territory in Europe and Africa. Since 1939 the nation had watched its traditional allies, Great Britain and France, vainly attempt to restrain the Nazi drive. As France, Belgium, the

Netherlands, Denmark, and Eastern Europe fell to the Nazis, American policy changed from neutrality to cautious support. But the legacy of the "war to end all wars" was powerful. It took a direct assault on a U.S. naval base, the Japanese attack on Pearl Harbor on the morning of December 7, 1941 for America to enter the war. Both before and after U.S. involvement, isolationists, pacifists, some immigrant groups, and a variety of right-wingers opposed the war effort.

Liberals and Leftist Radicals

Unlike World War I, which socialists and some liberals had denounced as a war fought to protect the investment of U.S. capitalists, nearly all left wingers supported American entry into World War II. All through 1940, the country's two leading liberal journals, *Nation* and *New Republic*, grew increasingly bellicose, supporting the Selective Service Act, calling men who refused to register "cowards and traitors" and carrying on a noisy campaign for suppression of isolationists and right wingers.

Socialists and their splinter groups had been the harshest critics of the first war, but from the moment Hitler invaded the Soviet Union in June 1941, they demanded U.S. intervention. The communists, who had split from the Socialist Party after World War I, were particularly enthusiastic war supporters, opposing strikes that might impede production of war materials and, ironically, calling for the suppression of antiwar critics. Their many publications, which a generation earlier had lashed out against U.S. policy and incurred the wrath of the U.S. government, were now devoted to encouraging the war effort.

Criticism from the Right

They were called "native fascists." Before Pearl Harbor they urged nonintervention. After December 1941, they charged that Jews and communists tricked the United States into the war. One of their leaders was the anti-Semitic radio demagogue Father Charles Coughlin whose magazine, *Social Justice*, attracted 200,000 subscribers. Considered by some historians as a journal of the "right-wing lunatic fringe," *Social Justice* called for "all Jews to retire from the field of politics and government." Coughlinite gangs roamed the streets of Boston attacking Jews and smashing storefronts of Jewish-owned businesses. In 1942 the Attorney General, citing the Espionage Act of 1917, asked the Postmaster General to suspend the magazine's second-class mailing privileges because it echoed the enemy's line and could damage troop morale. The government choose instead to silence Coughlin by applying pressure through the Catholic church. But 26 native fascists were indicted for spreading hatred against the Jews, fear of the communists, distrust of public officials, and undermining the war effort.

Charles Lindbergh, the quintessential culture hero of the 1920s, was blasted as an anti-Semitic fascist and a Nazi-loving traitor after a September 1941 speech in which he blamed the Jews for being "war agitators." But Lindbergh, who was an isolationist before Pearl Harbor and a war supporter after the attack, based his early opposition to the war on his sincere belief that the United States would be defeated. He had personally inspected German military bases and was convinced that Germany's military might far exceeded America's.

Pacifists

Before Pearl Harbor the pacifist movement was organizationally weak. Its main groups, the Fellowship of Reconciliation (FOR) and the War Resisters League (WRL), attracted few members and exerted virtually no political power. But the Selective Service Act of 1940 mobilized the movement. Membership in the WRL climbed to 12,000 and the FOR expanded to include a wide variety of Christian pacifists and Christian Socialists. The 1940 draft legislation allowed people with a sincere belief in religious teachings with a profound moral objection to war (essentially Quakers, Mennonites, and Brethren, the traditionally "peace churches") to be classified as conscientious objectors. Later draft legislation narrowed the CO category by insisting that objectors believe in a "transcendent creator-diety." More than 12,000 COs worked in civil public service camps; perhaps 80,000 accepted noncombatant service; 6,000, denied official CO status, went to prison.

Objectors and draft resisters who were not members of the three traditional peace churches had a difficult time qualifying for CO status. Vilified by the convention press—the *New York Times* called them "mindless, ignorant and arrogant," the liberal press called them cowards—pacifists depended on their own journals to support and clarify their antiwar philosophies and report on the pacifist movement.

Perhaps the most important of these journals was *The Conscientious Objector,* an eight-page monthly newspaper published by FOR and WRL volunteers. With a peak circulation of 4,000 but a readership of many thousands more, *The Conscientious Objector* covered the national and international pacifist movement, detailed the treatment of COs in work camps, publicized pacifist trials and legal battles, and acted as a national bulletin board for the movement. Editorials called for repeal of the Selective Service Act, an end to harassment of "enemy aliens," cautious treatment of the Japanese and an immediate negotiated peace. From October 1939 to June 1946, the newspaper urged its readers to remain true to their consciences.

Other anti-war journals sprang up to support the pacifist movement. *Retort,* an anarchist quarterly published in upstate New York, proclaimed its "uncompromising opposition to the war and militarism." *Resistance,* published from 1942 to 1952, counseled draft resistance and evasion. *The Arbitrator,* a New York monthly, carried the motto "to outlaw war" on its masthead. In California, *Pacifica Views* argued that "pacifism is the revolutionary movement of the 20th century" and attacked CO work camps as "forced labor programs." Radical journalist Dwight Macdonald, after resigning from the leftist but prowar *Partisan Review,* started his own iconoclastic antiwar journal, *Politics.* The *New York Call,* a famous socialist daily that had been silenced for its opposition to World War I, was a leader in the fight against conscription. Dorothy Day's *Catholic Worker,* an anarcho-pacifist newspaper founded in 1933, continued as a strong antiwar voice.

Alien Enemies

Because of twentieth-century immigration restriction, there were proportionately fewer immigrants in the United States during World War II than during World War I. Still, there were millions of Germans and Italians, including 850,000 who were not yet American citizens, and perhaps 130,000 Japanese, many of whom were not naturalized because the 1924 Immigration Act had made them ineligible for citizenship. The day after the United States declared war, Roosevelt declared all German, Italian, and Japanese noncitizens "enemy aliens." The executive order suspended all naturalization proceedings and restricted travel and employment. As in World War I, the government feared what the foreign-language press was telling its readers.

Prior to Pearl Harbor perhaps a dozen of the more than 150 German-language publications were openly pro-Nazi. While a few were violently anti-Nazi, most were noncommittal, attempting to avoid the issue of Nazism while maintaining their traditional anti-British attitude. Major German publications like the New York *Staas-Zeitung* and the Rochester *Abenpost* called for isolationism. But after Pearl Harbor, the few pro-Nazi publications quickly dropped out of sight, and the German-language press as a whole either supported the war or omitted all war-related news. However, the small but active German-American Bund continued to counsel draft resistance throughout the war.

In 1940 about 80% of Italian-language publications were profascist. The editor of New Haven's *Corriere del Connecticut* wrote that Italy was involved in a "holy war of liberation." Another editor called Mussolini's conquest of Ethiopia "another beautiful page in Italian history." The few antifascist newspapers were socialist, anarchist, or communist publications.

Although the Italian government did not become antifascist until mid-1944, the Italian-American press expressed its unequivocal loyalty to the United States following Pearl Harbor. The United Italian-American League, the Mazzini Society, and nearly all Italian-language publications were avid war supporters, encouraging Italian-Americans to enlist. Roosevelt was so impressed with Italian-American loyalty that he took Italians off the enemy alien list on Columbus Day 1942.

It was toward the Japanese that the U.S. government directed its most repressive policies. At the time of Pearl Harbor 112,000 Japanese were living on the West Coast. Many, because of the 1924 Immigration Act, were noncitizens and thus classified as "enemy aliens." West Coast Japanese were served by a number of daily and weekly newspapers published in cities from Seattle to Los Angeles. Reacting to strong racial prejudice, some Japanese editors had begun issuing English-language editions or including English sections in the mid-1920s. Japanese papers, attempting to give their readers a sense of community and pride amid racial hostility, stressed cultural rather than political news.

But after Pearl Harbor it seemed to make little difference whether Japanese residents or their newspapers were loyal to the American cause. "A Jap," said General John Dewitt, head of the West Coast Defense Command, "is a Jap. . . . It makes no difference whether he is an American citizen of not. . . . I don't want any of them." Three months after Pearl Harbor, the government ordered the evacuation of all Japanese from the West Coast. Commanded to leave their homes and settle "elsewhere," Japanese refugees soon discovered that few states wanted them. By September 1942 the War Relocation Authority had placed more than 100,000 Japanese in ten internment camps in seven western states. Japanese newspapers, along with all other Japanese-owned businesses, ceased to exist. The treatment of this immigrant group was the most blatant mass violation of civil liberties in American history.

The War and the Government

America congratulated itself that the hysterical excesses of World War I were not repeated in World War II. In fact, there were perhaps ten times as many victims of persecution in World War II as there had been in World War I. More than 100,000 Japanese were deprived of their civil rights; 18,000 Americans were prosecuted for draft evasion; 6,000 pacifists were jailed; 150 people were indicted under the Espionage Act; more than 100 publications (mostly from the extreme right wing) were suppressed; thousands were the victims of mob violence. The Office of War Information, with a first-year budget of $40 million and a staff of advertising copywriters, sold the war like a product. Japanese and Germans, wrote one historian of the period, were "stripped of their humanity" in a propaganda attempt to encourage 100% support for a war that many believed was as just as a war could be.

THE VIETNAM WAR

It was the most unpopular and least understood war in the history of the United States. During the Eisenhower and Kennedy administrations, few Americans even knew their country was involved in Southeast Asia. During the Johnson administration, few were aware of America's military tactics. When Americans finally began to understand what their country was doing in Vietnam—the bombing of nonmilitary targets, the napalming of villages and countrysides—millions joined the antiwar movement. At its heyday in the late 1960s and early 1970s, the movement included political leaders, clergy, students, GIs, traditional pacifists, assorted left wingers, a smattering of moderates, and hundreds of antiwar publications. But war resisters began their fight against U.S. involvement in Vietnam long before the cause became popular.

Early Antiwar Journalism

Throughout World War II, Korea, and the cold war, the *Catholic Worker* had promoted pacifism. In the early years of U.S. involvement in Vietnam, two decades before the antiwar press was born, Dorothy Day's Christian pacifist newspaper began its long fight against the Vietnam war. In 1948 it was joined by the *National Guardian,* an omnibus leftist publication founded by two professional newspapermen to back Progressive Party presidential candidate Henry Wallace.

From its inception, the *Guardian* began covering the developments in Vietnam, reporting on the postwar betrayal of the French and the defeat of the French army. With a peak of circulation of 100,000 and subscribers in small towns from Arkansas to Oregon—in addition to the traditional urban leftist audience—the *Guardian* was one of the few sources of independent (nongovernment) information about the war. In 1961 it sent veteran leftist journalist Anna Louise Strong to conduct an interview with Ho Chi Minh in which he correctly predicted the fall of Diem and the rise of anti-American sentiment. Beginning in 1963 it carried reports from special correspondent Wilfred Burchett, one of the few western journalists permitted to travel with the National Liberation Front. By mid-1963, the *National Guardian* was calling Vietnam "The Dirty War."

"The handwriting is on the wall for the U.S. misadventure in Vietnam," wrote *Guardian* editor James Aronson in early 1964. "The struggle may be long drawn, but this is a war the United States cannot win." In 1965, after Johnson ordered the bombing of North Vietnam, the *Guardian* carried stories about the destruction of hospitals, sanitariums, and farms. As the antiwar movement gained power through the last half of the 1960s, the newspaper covered demonstrations, marches, and speeches as well as continuing its international coverage.

A few years after the *Guardian* began publishing, iconoclastic journalist I. F. Stone founded *I. F. Stone's Weekly* as a one-man investigative journal. From 1953 to 1971 Stone singlehandedly wrote and edited the leftist weekly, keeping tabs on domestic politics, criticizing the conventional press, and speaking out against the war. He strongly defended antiwar activists' right to speak out. *Liberation,* established in 1956 by a group of independent radicals and pacifists including David Dellinger, Staughton Lynd, and Paul Goodman, was a leader in both the Black civil rights and antiwar movements. *Win*, a pacifist publication founded by the War Resisters League in 1965, published antiwar articles by Daniel Berrigan and antiwar poetry by Allen Ginsberg.

Another important antiwar voice was *Ramparts,* a small-circulation intellectual Catholic magazine that in 1965 became a popular leftist monthly. With a circulation of 250,000 in the late 1960s, *Ramparts* was the first popular periodical to reveal the extent and premeditation of U.S. involvement in Vietnam. It offered its readers firsthand reports of the killing and torturing of the Viet Cong, the effects of saturation bombing and racism in the military.

The New Antiwarriors

They were middle-class college and high school students who ignored the legacy of the Old Left to start their own movement and their own publications. In 1969 *Fortune* described them as "hippies and doctrinaire Leninists, anarchists and populists, the campus 'cong' and peaceful communards, militant confrontationists and mystics, Bakuninists and humanists, power seekers, ego trippers, revolutionaries, Maoists, rock bands and cultural guerrillas. . . . " With this diversity, it is no wonder they founded hundreds of so-called underground newspapers to further their causes. But whatever their individual aims, underground publications were vehemently and consistently against the war.

The number of underground papers published during the late 1960s and early 1970s is almost impossible to determine. Some published irregularly, many were short-lived, and none was registered with the Audit Bureau of Circulation. One chronicler of the underground press found 457 papers published in 41 states and the District of Columbia in 1970. The Underground Press Syndicate, an alternative news network founded in the late 1960s, estimated that it served 400 newspapers with a combined readership of 20 million in 1969.

Antiwar publications like the Chicago *Seed*, the Boston *Avatar*, the Philadelphia *Distant Drummer*, the San Francisco *Good Times*, the Berkeley *Barb*, and the Washington D.C. *Hard Times* covered peace marches and speeches, gave editorial support to the Viet Cong and North Vietnamese, offered radical interpretations of war events, and went on long tirades against U.S. imperialism. They were joined by alternative newspapers in every major American city from Atlanta to Seattle and in hundreds of college towns across the nation.

In addition to the underground press, which called for a revolution in lifestyles as well as an end to the war, there were a variety of publications that concentrated solely on Vietnam. *War Resisters League* and *Viet Report* in New York, *Counter-draft* in Los Angeles, *Conscientious Objector News Notes* in Philadelphia, *Peace and Freedom News* in Baltimore, and *Peace Brain* in Chicago were among these. Aiding the new antiwarriors in their fight—and perhaps even more important to the spirit of the movement—was the protest music of Pete Seeger, Joan Baez, Phil Ochs, Bob Dylan, and others.

The GI Antiwar Press

As the antiwar movement escalated with mass marches in New York, Chicago, and Washington, D. C., organized protest began on or near U.S. military bases. To be both in the military and against the war was a dangerous combination, and antiwar

GIs risked much in going public with their beliefs. It was a testament to the strength of their convictions—and a powerful statement on the war's unpopularity—that they did so. *The Bond: Voice of the American Servicemen's Union,* founded in Berkeley in 1967 and published in New York from 1968, was the first military antiwar newspaper. Claiming an international circulation of more than 100,000 by 1971, *The Bond* called for withdrawal of all troops, the right of military personnel to disobey what they considered illegal orders, and racial equality in the military. *The Ally,* a Berkeley-based newspaper started by a coalition of academics and ex-GIs, circulated throughout dozens of U.S. military bases at home and abroad.

By 1969 60 GI antiwar newspapers, including five internationally distributed publications, were being published on or near military bases. From Ft. Richardson, Alaska's *Anchorage Troop* to Ft. Hood, Texas' *Fatigue Press,* from Ft. Dix, New Jersey's *Ultimate Weapon* to Ft. Ord, California's *As You Were,* the GI protest press editorialized against the war, encouraged the organization of off-base antiwar coffeehouses, and provided news of both the civilian and military antiwar movements. Protest papers were published by military men in all four branches of the service.

Antiwar Protest and the Government

The alternative press was the target of "surveillance, harassment and unlawful search and seizure by U.S. government agencies," concluded leftist writer Geoffrey Rips after a three-year study of government documents obtained through the Freedom of Information Act. Cointelpro, a domestic spying program established by the FBI in 1956, planted scurrilous stories in the conventional press about war dissenters, opened mail, encouraged local police to harass dissidents, and infiltrated antiwar organizations, according to FBI documents. First aimed at Communist Party members, Cointelpro expanded its operation to include Blacks, pacifists, and antiwar leftists.

In 1967, at the behest of the Johnson administration, the Counter-Intelligence Division of the CIA initiated Operation Chaos. Purportedly designed to determine foreign influence in the antiwar movement, Operation Chaos included surveillance, disruption, and infiltration of antiwar groups. In 1968 FBI director J. Edgar Hoover sent a memo to all local offices instructing them to "immediately institute a detailed survey concerning New Left type publications..." and to send in reports detailing the names of the publications, their editorial staffs, their printers, and their sources of funds. In 1970, the Nixon administration created the Interagency Committee on Intelligence, which devised the Houston Plan, a program of electronic surveillance, break-ins, and infiltration of antiwar groups and their publications.

Cointelpro attempted to dissuade printers from printing antiwar publications. The FBI leaned on Columbia Records to stop advertising in underground newspapers. The Special Services Staff and Intelligence Divisions of the IRS cooperated by auditing the tax returns of and collecting confidential information on antiwar writers. Encouraged by federal agencies, local police attempted to disrupt the distribution of antiwar publications by rounding up street vendors and arresting them for vagrancy. Antiwar editors and writers were singled out in marijuana busts and were jailed on charges of pornography and inciting to riot.

GI antiwar editors and writers risked even more than their civilian counterparts. In addition to imprisonment, they were threatened with prosecution in military courts, demotions, and transfers to combat zones. The editor of Ft. Hood's *Fatigue Press* was sentenced to eight years for marijuana possession. At Ft. Ord, two soldiers were sentenced to four years in prison for distributing antiwar leaflets near the base.

In 1969 the Army issued its "Guidance on Dissent," stating that the "publication of underground newspapers by soldiers off post, and with their own money and equipment, is generally protected under the First Amendment." The on-base military command apparently paid little attention to the directive, and the harassment and intimidation continued until the end of the war.

"We Were Right"

Two years after the United States started bombing North Vietnam, the *New York Times* sent distinguished journalist Harrison Salisbury to Southeast Asia. "Contrary to the impression given by U.S. communiques, on-the-spot inspection indicates that American bombing has been inflicting considerable civilian casualties," wrote Salisbury, confirming what the antiwar press had been saying since the bombing began.

In 1971 when the *New York Times* published the Pentagon Papers, revealing the Johnson administration's deliberate and long-range war plans, the *East Village Other,* a countercultural, antiwar newspaper, wrote: "They called us every name in the book—fools, hippies, trippies and yippies—yet the fact remains, we were right."

REFERENCES

The following material aided in the preparation of this chapter and is suggested for further reading:

Armstrong, David. *A Trumpet to Arms: Alternative Media in America.* Los Angeles: J.P. Tarcher, 1981.

Belfrage, Cedric and Aronson, James. *Something to Guard: The Story Life of the National Guardian.* New York: Columbia University Press, 1978.

Blum, John. *V Was for Victory: Politics and American Culture during World War II.* New York: Harcourt Brace Jovanovich, 1976.

Brock, Peter. *Twentieth Century Pacifism.* New York: Van Nostrand Reinhold, 1970.

Conlin, Joseph R. *American Anti-War Movements.* Beverly Hills, CA: Glencoe Press, 1968.

Conlin, Joseph R. *The Radical American Press, 1880-1960,* Vol. II. Westport, CT: Greenwood Press, 1974.

Glessing, Robert. *The Underground Press in America.* Bloomington: Indiana University Press, 1970.

Knightly, Philip. *The First Casualty.* New York: Harcourt Brace Jovanovich, 1975.

Leamer, Laurence. *The Paper Revolutionaries.* New York: Simon & Schuster, 1972.

Middleton, Neil, ed. *The I. F. Stone's Weekly Reader.* New York: Random House, 1973.

Perrett, Geoffrey. *Days of Sadness, Years of Triumph: The American People 1939-1945.* New York: Coward, McCann and Geoghegan, 1973.

Peterson, H. C. and Fite, Gilbert. *Opponents of War 1917-1918.* Madison: University of Wisconsin Press, 1957.

Polenberg, Richard. *War and Society: The United States 1941-1945.* Philadelphia: J. B. Lippincott, 1972.

Rips, Geoffrey. *The Campaign Against the Underground Press.* San Francisco: City Lights Books, 1981.

8

THE JOURNALISTIC TRADITION OF RADICALISM

We will speak out, we will be heard,
Though all the earth's systems crack;
We will not bate a single word,
Nor take a letter back.
—James Russell Lowell

They did speak out. While the conventional press of the 1830s offered colorful human interest stories on urban life, Blacks and utopians spread their separate messages in newspapers of their own making. While Hearst amassed his empire in the late nineteenth and early twentieth centuries, feminists fought for their rights in the pages of their own journals, and immigrants built self-respect through their own publications. While the *New York Times* achieved major stature under Adolph Ochs in the first decades of the twentieth century, socialists and communists reached millions of discontented Americans through hundreds of journalistic outlets. While the conventional press called for and supported war throughout the twentieth century, war resisters disseminated their philosophy in the pages of their own publications.

The alternative press—the publications of political, social, cultural, and religious dissidents—has existed alongside the conventional media throughout American history. The dissident press is as much part of our journalistic heritage as the *New York Times, Chicago Tribune* and *Time* magazine. It is the forgotten chronicle of the ideas, goals, and actions of those at odds with the norms of their day.

THE DISSIDENT PRESS AND ACCESS

The mainstream press has traditionally spoken to and for the homogeneous middle. United by their belief in the current political, social, and cultural ideas of their day, the audiences of the conventional media receive a rather narrow spectrum of thought that reinforces these beliefs. Although the conventional media certainly report on controversy within the narrow spectrum—Democratic policies versus Republican policies, for example—the "fringe" ideas of dissidents are rarely covered.

Sometimes, as with Blacks, feminists, political leftists, and war resisters, it appears the conventional press purposefully excludes groups that go against the grain of contemporary society. In other cases—the utopians and immigrants, for example—the press seems to ignore groups because they do not fit into the current definition of what is news. When dissident groups receive coverage in the conventional press, as some obviously do at certain points in their history, the coverage is generally tied to some visible public act (a march or demonstration). The conventional media's event rather than issue orientation, although it holds true for both mainstream and fringe groups, it is particularly detrimental to dissidents. They need to define and communicate their ideas to a larger public as the first step toward meeting their goals (generally social or political change).

It was this need to communicate currently unacceptable ideas coupled with lack of access to the conventional press that led to the development of separate news channels for dissident groups. In many cases, it is clear that dissidents would have rather used the conventional press than start their own publications. Not only did the conventional press reach vast audiences with which the dissidents wished to communicate, it involved no extra expense. Most dissident groups were poor and poorly funded. Establishing and maintaining publications of their own was a major financial drain. They did so because they had to. As long as the conventional press continues to limit its scope to currently acceptable ideas and groups, as long as it defines news as action rather than thought, dissident groups will continue to support their own alternative media.

DISSIDENT JOURNALISTS

The men and women who devoted their time and energy to publishing dissident journals were people convinced of both the righteousness of their cause and the power of the press. They were malcontents who wanted change and idealists who believed change was possible. Many were simultaneously leaders and chroniclers of their cause.

They were both male and female; members of every racial, ethnic, and religious group represented in America. Coming from both urban centers and rural outposts, they lived and worked in every state of the union. Some were native born; others were immigrants. Some were wealthy, like Gaylord Wilshire, the "millionaire socialist"; others were poor, like Frederick Douglass who had to borrow money to buy his freedom. They were young, middle-aged, and old. Demographically, they were as varied a group as one could imagine, yet they had in common their devotion to a cause.

For the majority, journalism was not a separate calling or a profession for its own sake. It was a means to reach people with ideas, a way to organize and propagandize for what they believed. Publishing a newspaper or magazine was not the path to wealth; it was the path to a better world.

COMMON PROBLEMS

Some dissident journalists were harassed or ostracized by their communities. Some were harassed by the government. Some were jailed for their writings. But one problem all dissident journalists shared for all or most of their careers was how to continue financing their journalistic efforts. Most publications were started on a shoestring and remained financially unstable throughout their lifetimes.

Publishers had three potential sources of revenue: support from a group or individual, subscription and single-copy sales, and advertising income. Those able to rely on the financial support of a group were fortunate. *Woman's Journal* was funded by various suffrage clubs; *National Economist* was underwritten by the Texas Alliance; *The Daily Worker* received seed money from the Soviet Communist Party; several utopian journals were supported by the money-making ventures of experimental colonies. On extremely rare occasions, an outside "angel"—the wealthy eccentric who for two years supported Stanton and Anthony's *The Revolution*—might step in. But publications receiving financial support from dissident groups or outsiders were the exception. Most groups were resource-poor. Their members, often the poor, the powerless, and the disenfranchised, could not be counted on to contribute significant donations. What little money groups had they generally spent on organizing efforts.

Because in many cases those who would support a dissident publication were themselves impoverished, subscription and single-copy sales were generally not a successful way for journals to earn income. Women without an independent source of income, farmers who mortgaged their crops and land to stay in business one more year, utopians who gave up all personal assets when they joined a colony, and underpaid or unemployed workers often could not afford the price of the newspaper or magazine that supported their cause. The dissident press was full of pleas from editors facing creditors. Pay for your subscription now or this journal will be forced to stop publishing, wrote the editors. We need 100 (500, 1,000) more subscribers or we won't be able to stay in business, wrote others. Of course, there were notable exceptions. A handful of dissident publications had healthy circulations, and a few of the larger newspapers and magazines located in major urban areas could count on single-copy sales for some income.

Most of the conventional press depends on advertising revenue to sustain itself, but this was not an option for many dissident journals. Some flatly refused to carry advertising, claiming it would compromise their position. Many would have been glad to carry at least some kind of advertising, but they did not present an inviting audience to potential advertisers. Not only was the audience usually small, it was often comprised of readers who could not afford the goods and services advertisers had to sell. In most cases, advertising was limited to newspapers, magazines, and books that fell within the readers' field of interest.

With negligible financial support from groups and scant income from subscriptions and advertising, publishers of most dissident journals supported their efforts by dipping into whatever personal savings they had, borrowing from friends, using their printing facilities to do outside work, or holding down second jobs. Publishing a dissident journal was not a way to get rich. In fact, for many it was a road to poverty.

THE ROLE OF THE DISSIDENT PRESS

Most dissident publications attempted to communicate both internally to a group of believers and externally to those not converted to the cause. Intragroup communication gave those involved in the cause a sense of unity and purpose. Before national transportation and communication networks were developed, dissidents separated by geography but united by ideology established and maintained essential links through the pages of their publications. Here they could argue and discuss ideas, ask questions, receive advice, and read about the activities of fellow dissidents. They could learn about and participate in organizational matters. When it appeared they were in the midst of a losing battle, when they were harassed, ridiculed, or ostracized by their own communities, they could look to the pages of their journals for inspiration and comfort. Their publications showed them they were not alone.

In their role as external communicators, dissident journals attempted to perform two major functions: educate the "unconverted" public by presenting a forum for ideas generally ignored by the conventional press, and persuade the unconverted that their cause was righteous and worth supporting. Here the dissident press encountered its greatest obstacle, for, in general, it was read by those who were already supporters, not by those whom it wanted to convert. Successful, large-circulation dissident journals—several of the socialist and Populist publications, for example—were read by supporters and those most likely to become sympathetic (not yet converted urban workers or impoverished farmers). But both large- and small-circulation dissident publications were rarely read by those in power or those who had the power to effect change. This was partly because, as communications theory tells us, people tend to seek out those messages they already believe in (selective exposure). Partly it was because most dissident journals were shoestring operations that could not mount the circulation and promotion campaigns necessary to make themselves known to those outside their circle.

Despite those obstacles, some dissident publications were able, over time, to help groups "go public" with their ideas. These were groups whose ideas were ahead of, but not in the long run inimical to, the society in which they lived. Blacks and women fighting for enfranchisement and equality, immigrants fighting for acceptance and respect, workers fighting for the right to unionize, antiwar activists speaking out against Vietnam—the ideas of all these groups, first articulated in the dissident press, eventually found their way into both conventional media and mainstream society. For these dissidents, a press of their own was a starting point. Early on it helped them delineate their ideas and set up effective organizational structures. It provided a small forum for ideas most Americans were not yet willing to accept. Without a voice of their own, these groups might not have been able to grow strong enough to effect change. Their ideas might have taken even longer to find their way into mainstream thought.

But other dissident groups encountered an even greater obstacle: Their ideas were truly antithetical to the American way of life. Even if a publication were able to make itself known in wider circles, even if unsympathetic nonbelievers occasionally exposed themselves to dissident messages, some ideas did not and would never appeal to more than a small segment of the population. Utopianism, Populism, socialism, anarchism, communism, and pacifism (during the two world wars) attacked the basic American beliefs of private ownership, consumerism, competition, the role of the government, and the mission of the United States. These dissidents could—and did—publish thousands of journals explaining their beliefs and attempting to convert others, but their causes would never become popular.

Regardless of what they had to say or whether Americans wanted to hear it, dissident groups have had the constitutional right to speak and publish. When they were harassed and their publications repressed, the First Amendment rights of all Americans were in danger. When dissident ideas were routinely excluded from the mainstream press and relegated to the pages of poorly funded, small-circulation journals, freedom of speech lost its meaning. For when the framers of the Constitution talked of freedom of speech, they did not mean the freedom to talk to oneself. They meant both the freedom to speak *and* the opportunity to be heard.

ABOUT THE AUTHOR

Lauren Kessler is Assistant Professor at the University of Oregon School of Journalism, where she teaches communications history, mass media, and society and reporting. She has written several articles on communications history and co-authored *When Words Collide: A Journalist's Guide to Grammar and Style*. A magazine writer and former newspaper reporter, she received her Ph.D. from the University of Washington.